ALL GALL

Malicious Monologues

&

Ruthless Recitations

adapted from the French
by

Norman R. Shapiro

illustrated by
David Schorr

APPLAUSE
NEW YORK • LONDON

Permissions
Bernard, Tristan , "Le Lion" and "Les Médecins spécialistes," by arrangement with M. Nicolas Bernard and the Société des Gens de Lettres de France
Carrington, Leonora, "La Débutante": in *La Débutante*,
© Flammarion, Paris, 1978
Laclaverine, Jean-Marie, "Djinn": in *Le Rouge et le blanc*,
© Editions Gallimard, Paris, 1994
Raynaud, Fernand, "Ma sœur at son chapeau": in *Heureux!*,
© Editions de La Table Ronde, Paris, 1975
Sternberg, Jacques, "L'Hygiène": in *Histoires à mourir de vous*, ©Denoël, Paris, 1991
_____, "L'Horticulteur," "Le Tricot," "La Survie": in *Histoires à dormir sans vous*,
© Denoël, Paris, 1990
_____, "Le Marathon," "Le Répétitif": in *Contes griffus*,
© Denoël, Paris, 1993

Library of Congress Cataloging-in-Publication Data

Library of Congress Catalogue Card Number: 99-069413

British Library Cataloging-in-Publication Data

A catalogue Record of this book is available from the British Library

Applause Books
1841 Broadway Suite 1100
New York, NY 10023
Phone (212) 765-7880
Fax: (212) 765-7875
First Applause Printing 2000

Combined Book Services
Units I/K Paddock Wood Dist. Centre
Tonbridge Kent TN12 6UU
Phone: (44) 01892 837171
Fax: (44) 01892 837272

This collection, divided into four parts unlike the three of Caesar's Gaul, is aimed at two basic audiences: those who, with a sense of humor as twisted as my own—and especially fond of the Gallic manifestations thereof—will relish it for its literary interest, spanning, as it does, a variety of authors and styles, and of tones from the merely mischievous to the downright macabre; and those theatrical folk who, always on the lookout for fresh and novel audition materials—particularly those actors whose taste and talent veer toward the offbeat—will be pleased not to have to dig into the traditional, well-worn repertory of monologue scenes from this or that dramatic chestnut. Some, in search of unusual solo performance pieces, may even find a few here worth considering.

Two-pronged in aim, the materials are likewise twofold in origin: on the one hand, *bona fide* examples of the once popular monologue genre—practiced by the likes of Georges Feydeau, Fernand Raynaud, et al.—that flourished in France, in almost epidemic proportions, especially around the turn of the century, and that lives on, in spirit if not in style, in night club and TV—intended, *ipso facto*, to be heard; and, on the other, works intended primarily for the printed page, whether the brief journalistic vignettes of an Alphonse Allais, the modern prose poems of a Jacques Sternberg, or the lengthier fictions of an Apollinaire, a Villiers de l'Isle-Adam, and their literary confreres. For the printed page, perhaps. But, to be read in silence? Believing as I do that, in essence, all (yes, all) literature is meant to be heard—or should be—even if only in our heads, I see no contradiction whatever in freeing those latter works from the straitjacket of print and offering them here as pieces worthy to be recited *viva voce*. (Or, more appropriately, *à haute voix...*) And even demanding to be, for their fullest artistic realization.

The French have long loved what, for better or worse, has come to be known as *humour noir*, "black humor." The several dozen works in this collection will, I hope—whatever other practical purposes they may serve—help to show why. Perhaps they will also make a few converts to Gallic (and gall-ic) wit among my otherly-humored Anglo-American readers. And, of course, ideally, my listeners.

Norman R. Shapiro, *Cambridge, Massachusetts*

Acknowledgments

My thanks to the many friends and associates who, since the inception of this collection, have been helpful and supportive in a variety of ways: Lillian Bulwa, Robert Gorman, Scott Hamilton, Robert and Jana Kiely, Chuck Kim, Sylvia and Allan Kliman, Vicki Macy, Tamar March, Tom Moore, Gloria Ornstein, Seymour O. Simches, Franklin Smith, Maureen Spofford, and Caldwell Titcomb.

Lenore Gouyet has been especially generous with her time and research talents, as has Evelyn Singer Simha, with her gracious suggestions and her unerring aesthetic judgment. To them, my deep appreciation for their efforts.

A word of gratitude also to the several performers and directors—H. Stuart Shifman, Peter Stein, Dudley Knight, Winsome Browne, Richard Iain Nash-Sedlecky, Michael C. Haney—who have already proven the theatrical potential of many of these pieces.

And my special thanks to Glenn Young and Paul Sugarman of Applause Theatre and Cinema Books, for their patience, as well as to my colleague David Schorr, for his graphic talents and his sprightly illustrations.

Publication of this work has been aided by a grant from the Thomas and Catharine McMahon Fund of Wesleyan University, established through the generosity of the late Joseph McMahon.

Table
of
Contents

I

Of Mischief, Malice, Murder,
& the Law

Capital Crime, Parisian Punishment   1
by Georges Feydeau

In the Game of the Law   7
by Georges Feydeau

Righteous You Are If You Think You Are   14
by Georges Feydeau

The Lawyers and the Lady, or All's Fair in Love and Law   18
by Eugène Chavette

The Volatile Mother-in-Law, or Science to the Rescue   29
by Alphonse Allais

Widow's Pique, or After the Fall   32
by Alphonse Allais

Cream and Punishment   39
by Alphonse Allais

Disorder in the Court   43
by Léon Xanrof

Bag and Baggage   46
by Tristan Bernard

The Last Laugh   51
by Alexandre Breffort

Clean Out of Her Mind   56
by Jacques Sternberg

Love in Bloom   58
by Jacques Sternberg

II

Of Ills, Potions, Cures, Quacks,
& Saviors

The Heroic Deed of Doctor Hallidonhill,   63
or Conspicuous Consumption
by Auguste de Villiers de l'Isle-Adam

Great Expectorations, or T.B. or Not T.B.   68
by Alphonse Allais

The Germ of the Problem   71
by Alphonse Allais

Patient Cure Thyself, or The Unkindest Cut of All   74
by Léon Xanrof

Double Crossed   77
by Léon Xanrof

Medic-à-la-Mode, or A Modern Surgeon's
New Cures for Old Ills   84
by Tristan Bernard

Woes Be Gone, or A Druggist's Young Wife Writes Home   87
by Tristan Bernard

Weight for the Doctor, or Reductio ad Absurdum   90
by Tristan Bernard

Orange Aid, or Curious Cure, Curious Doctor   94
by Guillaume Apollinaire

Belly-Hoo, or Doctors Sew-and-Sew   98
by Gabriel de Lautrec

III

Of Torsos, Limbs, Skulls, & Assorted Body Parts

The English Tongue   103
by Maurice Mac-Nab

The Blemished Bride, or The Seat of the Problem   105
by Maurice Mac-Nab

Till Death Do Them Part   109
by Alphonse Allais

A Lover's Cool Feat   114
by Alphonse Allais

Melt Down, or The Case of the Migrating Petrolatum   117
by Alphonse Allais

Split Decision, or The Blade, the Maid, and the Blade   121
by Alphonse Allais

Dressing to Kill   124
by Alphonse Allais

To Break a Bed Habit   127
by Alphonse Allais

Just for Malpractice   130
by Léon Xanrof

Ethnic Cleansing 1900: A Fool and His Mania,
or Dyeing Can Be Fatal   133
by Edouard Osmont

To Serve One's Fellows, or A Ship of Foods   140
by Tristan Bernard

Of Arms—Eyes, Mouths, Noses—and the Man   143
by Guillaume Apollinaire

The Disappearance of Honoré Subrac, or Point Blank   147
by Guillaume Apollinaire

Ahead and Behind   153
by Francis Picabia

The Debutante, or Defaced   155
by Leonora Carrington

Knit-Wit, or The Thread of the Story   161
by Jacques Sternberg

IV

Of Death and Dying:
Ways & Means, Whys & Wherefores

Of Tombs and Blooms   164
by Auguste de Villiers de l'Isle-Adam

Of Waiter, Wine, and Water, or A Buoyant Experience   166
by Alphonse Allais

From Collection to Collation, or A Consuming Passion Consumed   171
by Alphonse Allais

Money Is Time, or The Poor Beggar and the Good Fairy   176
by Alphonse Allais

The Fatal Inflection   181
by Léon Xanrof

Rogue Rug, or Mourning Prayer   187
by Tristan Bernard

Saint Adorata, or The Back Door to Heaven   189
by Guillaume Apollinaire

Requiesc-Hat, or A Grave Mistake   194
by Fernand Raynaud

Behind Closed Doors, or Of Tide and Time   199
by Jacques Sternberg

Over and Over... and Over   202
by Jacques Sternberg

Quo Vadis? or The Marathon   204
by Jacques Sternberg

Bottled Up, or The Genie   206
by Jean-Marie Laclavetine

The Authors   214

Bibliography *&* sources   222

I

Of Mischief, Malice, Murder,
&
the Law

Capital Crime, Parisian Punishment

Me! Sentenced to Death!... And at my age, too!... So young, so bright, so handsome... (*He sighs.*) Ah! At least... (*Raising his eyes to heaven.*) At least He'll know the truth... When you're going to meet your maker, you owe Him that much... Me! Sentenced to death! And no time off for good behavior... Well, let Posterity be the judge...

And by whom, I ask you! By whom?... By the Gentlemen of the Jury, that's by whom!... Can you imagine?... A pack of nobodys... Really, who are they?... A bunch of butchers and bakers... Grocers, for heaven's sake!... Believe me, if you owed them money they'd never find you guilty!... They're no fools!... It's disgusting, that's what it is... Disgusting!...

Well, that's why I'm here... Because those Gentlemen of the Jury were out for my neck... A neck is a neck, no matter how you slice it... Me, with such a good head on my shoulders... For now, that is... Until one of these mornings, when they come wake me up, to put me to sleep... Forever... At dawn, I suppose... And to think, they say: "Early to bed, early to rise, makes a man healthy..." (*He shakes his head.*) Then they'll tell me I can smoke, and they'll take me to the guillotine... Me! So young, so bright, so handsome... Ah! Sometimes it's not easy to keep your head, believe me...

My lawyer says only the President can save me now... "Clemency" he calls it... If I sign an appeal... A life sentence, if I'm lucky... Instead of a death sentence, that is... "Take your choice," he tells me... Well, I didn't think twice. I've always thought living was nicer than dying... Ever since I was a baby... So I signed the appeal...

But I don't have much hope. They tell me my case is too horrible for words... The crime of the century... "The defendant is accused of murdering his aunt, at night, by moonlight, after which he cut off her left breast, in cold blood..." Now I ask you... Murdering your aunt is one thing, but her left breast... Why on earth... If any of you ever murdered your aunt, did you cut off her left breast? I mean, really...

Well, it seems that's just what somebody did. Somebody... But not me... It's a miscarriage of justice, that's what it is... Yes, talk about miscarriages...

Let me tell you... I was born thirty years ago... Well, going on thirty... In my home town... Montpellier... That is, it's my home town, but I wasn't really born there. Actually I was born on a train... A sleeping-car... I'd never set foot on a train before... Mamma was in an upper berth... Me too... And Papa? You're probably wondering about Papa... I wondered too... And so did Mamma... For nine months she wondered... Well anyway, there she was in her upper... An all at once, pow!... She said that was one berth she'd never forget...

Well, being born on a train and all, you'd think I'd be quite a traveler. I mean, with a start like that... But I'm not... In fact, thirty years, and I'd never seen Paris... Going on thirty, that is... So one day I said to myself: "Do you realize you're going on thirty and you've never seen the capital?" "Well," I answered, "there's only one way to see it. You've got to go there!" So one, two, three, I made up my mind. I remember, it was a Friday... The thirteenth of August... It was only the second train I'd ever set foot on... In thirty years... Well, going on... And I said to myself: "I'll go visit Aunt Eglantine while I'm there. She lives on one of those fancy boulevards, across from the Courthouse. I'll drop in and surprise her. I'm sure she'll be delighted. Why not? A nephew like me... So young, so bright, so handsome..."

The next day I get to Paris. As soon as I'm out of the station, I ask someone: "Which way to the boulevard where the Courthouse is?" "Easy," he tells me. "There's a bus that goes there direct." Sure enough, on the next corner, what do I see but a bus, all painted black, standing in front of a shop that's got a kind of lantern hanging outside with "Police" written on it. So I ask someone: "Does this bus go to the Courthouse?" "Damn right," he tells me, "it's the paddy-wagon!" So I say to myself: "Just what I'm looking for!" And I get on the bus. That is, actually you could say I sneak on, because I figure if all those people are waiting for it too, I'll never get a seat... Anyway, I get on, and sit down, and wait...

In the meantime all the people outside are still talking... Jabbering away.... And I can hear them saying things like: "They say he murdered his aunt... At night... By moonlight... And then he cut off her left breast... In cold blood..." Well, naturally, I figure they're talking about some crime or other... You know, a highwayman... Out in the country... That sort of thing... But before I know it, they're all running every which way, and everyone's yelling and screaming: "Arrest him, arrest him!..." So I stick my head out the window and I ask someone: "What's happening?..." Well, what do you think?... The bus driver turns around... He's wearing a fancy blue uniform... With stripes, no less... And he's carrying a sword... A saber, if you can believe it... Anyway, he turns around and sees me, and he yells out at the top of his lungs: "My God! He's in the wagon!..." Some bus driver! I found out later he was in the National Guard... A soldier, of all things... Damn! All I can say is there must be an awful lot of soldiers in Paris if they use them to drive buses!...

Well, when things settle down we get ready to leave... As soon as we're moving I go over to the conductor... Like anybody would do, right?... And I tell him: "If you don't mind, my good man, you can let me off just before the Courthouse. That's my stop..." And I go to pay my fare with a handful of change... A few centimes, not enough to make a fuss... Well, "fuss" isn't the word! He stops the bus... A policeman shows up... And what does the driver tell him? That I tried to "buy him off," or something like that... With a few centimes? Really!... Well, they swear out a warrant against me, then and there... "Attempted corruption of a public official"... And the policeman praises the conductor for his "outstanding conduct"... (*With a shrug.*) A conductor, after all... For not letting himself be bribed... I suppose that's one driver who'll get himself a promotion. And why? Because I tried to pay my fare, and asked him to let me off just before the Courthouse!… Can you imagine?… Well, after all that you'd think the least they'd do would be to stop so I could see my aunt… "You'll see her all right!" the policeman told me. "You'll see her at the station… What's left of her, that is…"

Next thing I know, I'm standing in front of the judge. Before I can even open my mouth he tells me: "No use denying it, we know what happened. You murdered your aunt, at night, by moonlight, and you cut off her left breast!" Well, you can just imagine…

Then he tells me: "And now, monsieur, you'll please be so good as to tell us how you killed her!"

"But what are you talking about? I don't even know the woman!"

"Don't know your aunt? Come, come now, monsieur!"

"But she's not my aunt!"

"Oh? And how can you be sure, if you say you don't know her?"

"Because I know my own aunt, that's how! My aunt…"

"Tsk tsk, monsieur… You just told us you didn't! Please! Make up your mind!… I suppose you deny that you cut off her left breast too?"

"Of course I deny it! Even more!"

"Even more, monsieur? More that what? More than killing her? You mean that you don't deny killing her as much?"

"I do! Of course I do! It's just that, when it comes to my aunt's breasts, Your Honor… There's nothing to cut… She's flat as a board… They're nothing but padding…"

"Aha! And precisely how, may I ask, were you able to ascertain that the objects in question, belonging to your aunt, are 'nothing but padding'?"

"Because it runs in the family. We're all flat as a board... Especially the women..."

"No, no, monsieur! I'm sorry to contradict you! Your late aunt's are hardly padding! They're flesh and blood, my friend! Flesh and blood!... Unless, of course, you presume to know more than our coroners!... No, no! That line of defense won't save you! 'I cut off her breast because I thought it was only padding...' Ha! Padding indeed!"

"But..."

"No, no, monsieur! We've heard quite enough..."

Then they bring in a witness, and he swears he saw me do it. After all, that's what witnesses are for... To swear they saw you do it when you get yourself arrested... And just like that, they charge me...

There I am, telling the judge: "But I didn't... I didn't..." And finally he says: "Deny it all you want, monsieur! You'll rot in a cell until you decide to confess!"

Well, what could I do? I didn't have much choice. So I confessed... "You see? You see?" the judge yelled. "I told you! Maybe now you'll believe me... All right, tell us what you did with it!"

"With what?"

"With her breast!... Her breast!..."

That did it. I don't know what got into me, but all of a sudden I saw red, and I told him: "I ate it, goddammit!"

Well, that was my downfall. Once it was out there was no

taking it back. I'd eaten my aunt's left breast, and that was that...

Then nothing to do but wait for the trail.

My lawyer was a nice young man... Very happy-go-lucky... He says to me: "Look, there's no point your pleading not guilty... Really... They'll never believe you... I'm going to plead extenuating circumstances... That way, with luck, we could get off with life... At hard labor..." Now that's what I call luck!

You should have seen all the people at the trial. You wouldn't believe it... And the prosecutor, who kept telling the jury: "The death penalty is too good for him!... Too good... Too good..." I agree. I don't deserve it...

My lawyer defended me the best he could. He said I wasn't really such a terrible criminal... After all, I only ate one breast when I could have eaten two! But the prosecutor told them that didn't prove a thing. Not that I wasn't a big criminal, anyway... Only that I had a small appetite, that's all. And before I knew it they found me guilty... Sentenced to death on three counts, no less... One, for murdering my aunt. Two, for cutting off her left breast. And three, for eating it... But my lawyer says not to worry... They can only kill me once...

Now only the President of the Republic can save me! (*Apostrophising.*) Ah! Monsieur... Monsieur... Don't let an innocent victim suffer!... After all, maybe some day you'll be sentenced to death too, for eating your aunt's left breast... You never know... Don't deprive society of a person like me... So young, so bright, so handsome... Mercy, monsieur! Mercy!... Ah! Monsieur... Monsieur... Monsieur...

Georges Feydeau, *Un Monsieur qui est condamné à mort*

In The Game of the Law

(*Shouting into the wings.*) That's right! I'm not at home!... Not for anybody, understand?... (*He begins to come downstage, but turns back toward the wings.*) Except for reporters... Or defendants' relatives... (*To the audience.*) That's what I said!... When you take your job seriously, you should give it your all. Especially a responsible job, like mine... You see, I'm a juror... A member of the jury... A juryman... Right now, that's all that matters. Everything else can wait.

And just think... A week ago, what was I?... I'll tell you. I was a jeweler, that's what... That is, I still am, but... You understand... Today, juryman first and jeweler second... There I was, with a nice little business of my own... Just minding my own business... Next thing you know, Fate taps me on the shoulder, and now I'm a juror. Holding a human life in my hands... Well, one twelfth of a life, considering... Here, in these two hands... The power of life and death... And if I don't like the poor beggar's looks, or if I've got indigestion... (*He mimes slitting his throat.*) Me!... A juror in the Criminal Court of Paris! Whoever would have thought...

Vive la Justice!

But don't misunderstand... I don't take it that lightly. Nothing frivolous about my verdicts... Not me... I appreciate the awesome responsibility of my position. That's why I do like no other juror, past or present... You see, for each case I sit on, I invite the defendant's relatives to come talk, and tell me all about him... Because there's no better way to find out about someone than to talk to the people who know him best!... That's right... Straight from the horse's mouth... Or at least the horse's family... And it works too, believe me!

If the other jurors did it... If they talked to relatives and heard the things I hear... Well, it wouldn't take them long to learn one important basic fact: that it's only the innocent who are ever found guilty!... It's a scandal! Really!... We've got to do something about it!...

The trouble is that most jurors don't take their job seriously. That's right... Not like me... Yesterday, for example... I overheard a couple of them talking outside the courtroom. About some assassin... An Englishman, I think... And one of them asked the other:

"So, what if he was put on trial here, and if you were on the jury? How would you vote?"

"Oh, I don't know... How about you?"

"That's not fair! I asked you first!"

"Well, maybe I'd flip a coin..."

Then the first one says:

"You know, somebody told me they're sure he's going to hang... That is, if they ever catch him!"

"Then I guess I'd find him guilty," the second one says.

"Me too! After all, he wouldn't hang if he was innocent..."

You see? That's what I mean... Heads or tails!... That's how seriously most jurors take their job. They'll flip a coin and send the poor soul to the gallows. But no one ever thinks about talking to his relatives! Tsk tsk tsk!... No one but me... Oh, the Englishman's name, by the way... Not that it matters, but it's Ripper... Jack Ripper... (*With a shrug.*) Or something like that...

The problem is that most of the time they're just not logical. That's right... They don't use their heads... Their common sense... Take the other day, for instance. They let this absolutely vicious, depraved criminal get off with a slap on the wrist... Three measly years in prison... A barbarian who smashed in three jewelry shop windows and made off with a bundle!... Now I ask you... Three years? Really!... For three jewelry shops?... That's roughly one year per shop, heaven help us!... If they asked me, I'd have sent that swine to the guillotine! After twenty or thirty years at hard labor!... Just as an example!... A bakery I wouldn't mind. Let him smash in all the windows he likes. But a jewelry shop? And three of them?... Good God! Three years?... I'm telling you... (*Sighing.*) Some jurors...

On the other hand, the same day, they sentence a man to death. Some poor devil from the slums... Why? Because he has the nasty habit of knifing all the sixty-year-old women in the neighborhood and ripping them up the middle... That's right... (*Tapping his forehead.*) I admit he has a problem... But sentence him to death?... Not me! What do I care if he knifes all the sixty-year-old women? And in the slums, no less!... Do I live in the slums? Am I sixty years old?... No, and I'm not a woman!... So?...

No... You see, to be a good juror and to give the right verdict, you have to ask yourself a question: What's the nature of the crime? Is it social or individual? Does it harm the society at large, or doesn't it?... For example, let's say a man kills his wife... Or his mother-in-law... Or both... Now, obviously, that isn't a crime against society. I mean, I can say to myself: "If I run into him tomorrow, is my life going to be threatened? Am I in any danger?... No! Of course not!... So, someone like that you let off with a slap on the wrist. That's right... But a madman who smashes in jewelry shop windows? Oh no! Off with his head! Tomorrow it could be my turn! No, thank you!... Besides, that's what you call a crime against society!... I mean, not everyone has a wife... Or a mother-in-law... But everyone wears jewelry of one kind or another, sometime in their life... Really, like I say... Just a little common sense...

Or suppose that a criminal holds up a bank and he gets away with millions... Well, I don't have to tell you how much interest there would be... Or say he swindles a capitalist... Some big financier... All right, how should they sentence him?... (*He pauses.*) Wrong!... A slap on the wrist!... Why? Because that's the kind of crime that does society some good!... It keeps the economy healthy... Doesn't let it stagnate... Keeps the money moving, if you know what I mean... No, give him a week or two, at the most... Just to cover the law... That way he can get out and keep up the good work...

It's that sort of thing that most jurors don't grasp. That's right... The subtleties... The little ins and outs... I mean, I see how they act every day, believe me. I know what I'm talking about!... Like those two I was just mentioning... Heads or tails, remember?... Most of them don't have the faintest idea what their verdict is going to be... Not until the trial... After they've heard all the testimony... Really!... I know! It's unbelievable!... Imagine! They sit there and listen to every blessed word! Through the whole trial, mind you... And then, after all that talk, talk, talk, they try to decide if he's innocent or guilty! As if the trial is the time or place for such decisions!... A verdict is too important to put it off until the trial! Who can think straight with everybody swearing this and swearing that!... Why, it wouldn't surprise me, with all that confusion, if some day they found the judge himself guilty!...

Well, with my system it's different. It's perfectly logical. First I read all the newspapers, then I average their opinions. That way, when I come to the trial I'm all ready. No chance I can get confused... Each side can prove whatever they like... It doesn't matter... I've got my verdict and I'll stick to it, thank you! They're not going to sway me with all their fancy speeches! That's all we need! More indecisive jurors!... Otherwise, just think... I mean, a criminal comes in... He proves beyond a doubt that he's as innocent as a lamb... Pure as the driven snow... Now, all of a sudden, you're confused... You're troubled... You don't know what to do... You're pulled this way and that... And finally you give in. You forget what the papers said. You forget that public opinion has already found him guilty... That's right... Public opinion!... What higher court is there?... And so you let him off. You acquit him!... It's disgusting!...

If you don't believe me... Well, take this case, yesterday, for example. Very minor... No publicity at all... Not one word about it in any of the papers... So, naturally, there was no way I could use my system. No choice but to listen to all the testimony... All the talk, talk, talk!... I mean, what else could I do?... Just like the other jurors... There we were, in the jury room, all looking at each other... "Guilty!... Innocent!... Innocent!... Guilty!..." Half and half... Right down the middle... An absolute stalemate... That's when one of the jurors said: "Listen, someone is just going to have to change his vote!..." Everyone agreed, but nobody wanted to be the one. Then I said: "Look, it's not right to force anyone. Let's be fair... Let's all change..." And we did, but it didn't help... So we made up our minds we would leave it to chance. We'd each draw a card and let the high man decide... Well, I'll tell you, that defendant can thank his lucky stars that somebody had an ace!... That's right... Because I had a king, and believe me, if it was high... (*He mimes slitting his throat.*) But no... (*Sighing.*) He was acquitted...

Anyway, from now on they won't catch me napping, newspapers or not. Tomorrow we're hearing a sensational case... A real crime of passion... (*As if reading the headlines.*) "Jealous husband decides to kill wife's lover... Waits for him in doorway... When victim arrives, husband stabs him in chest with scissors..." Whew! "Passion" is right!... There's only one problem... Unfortunately, once he's gone and stabbed him, the husband stands back, takes one look, and he screams: "My God! It's not him!" It seems that the man with the scissors in his chest isn't the lover at all... He's a process-server... Just one of the other tenants, who was coming home for dinner!... Talk about being in the wrong place at the wrong time!... Some people... Which only goes to show that a husband should always be sure to count to ten before he stabs his wife's lover in the chest with a pair of scissors!... The poor murderer mutters an excuse, as best he can: "Sorry, monsieur... But I thought you were someone else..." Yes... No doubt... Tsk tsk tsk!... The process-server dies on the spot... Without saying a word... But it's clear from the look on his face what he's thinking: "Perhaps so, monsieur. But I do wish you'd found out sooner!..." Unless, maybe, it means: "Oh? Damn! Of all times! Just when I was having some friends in for dinner!" I mean, looks can be deceiving... It's hard to tell exactly...

Well, at any rate, that's the man who goes on trial tomorrow… No time to read the papers… So, innocent or guilty? How should I find him?… This morning I discussed it with the family… My wife, that is… And her mother… And her cousin, who lives with us… A very distant cousin, but a cousin… And Etienne, my valet… I asked for their advice… Well, to begin with, my mother-in-law really got on my nerves. She's not exactly the easiest person to get along with! So, what does she tell me? I'll tell you what she tells me! She says: "If you were a man, you would find him guilty! But you're not, so you won't!" "Not a man?" I answered. "Listen, you old… I'll show you who's a man!… I'll tell them to draw and quarter him goddammit! I'll show you…"

My wife calmed me down. She thinks he's guilty too. She said any man who would kill his wife's lover can't be anything but guilty! Her cousin agreed… Maybe just to please her… He's terribly devoted… Anyway, he said: "Yes, I think he's guilty too! After all, if every husband went and killed his wife's lover, just like that… Well, what would become of us?…" Etienne thought just the opposite. "I'd let him off!" he told me. "When a husband tries to kill his wife's lover, and he manages to get rid of a process-server in the bargain, I think that's pretty neat!" And who can disagree? I mean, one process-server more or less… Really! Who's going to miss him?…

No… The husband is innocent! Whose fault is it that someone was stealing his wife? His? No!… What was he supposed to do? Just sit back and let him take her?… In King Solomon's day it would have been easy… They'd have taken his "better half" and slit her in two! Half for him, half for the lover… (*With a little laugh.*) Two "better quarters"… Then at least he'd still have his half… Better or worse… But today we don't do that any more. Today it's all or nothing!

Well, my mind is made up. I know how I'm going to vote… Not guilty!… That's right… And if I were his lawyer, I know what I'd tell the jury… Me and all the others. Not that the other jurors would understand, but still… I'd say: "Gentlemen of the jury, in all good conscience you cannot find my client guilty!… What is the charge?… Premeditated murder!… Ah, but consider the facts!… On the one hand, it's true that my client, indeed, meant to kill his wife's lover. But did he? Did he kill him?... No! In point of fact he did not!... So, gentlemen of the jury, where, then is the murder?... On the other hand, my client did, indeed, kill a process-server. But did he mean to kill him?... No! In point of fact he did not!... So, gentlemen of the jury, where, then, is the premeditation?... I rest my case. This man is not guilty as charged!"

That's what I'd tell them... "Us," I mean... The other jurors and me... Because, frankly, the way I see it... Well, there's only one person who's guilty in all this... One person who's responsible for the husband's revenge... For the fact that there's one less process-server in the world... If you're going to send anyone to the guillotine, my friends, it should be the wife's lover! He started it all!

My wife's cousin doesn't think so. But then, he's never been a juror...

Georges Feydeau, *Le Juré*

Righteous You Are If You Think You Are

You say you've never seen any idiots?

Well, take a look at me... I've seen more than you can shake a stick at, believe me!

A couple of days ago, for example, I was at the theater. They were doing *Hamlet*... Great, let me tell you!... It was so great, in fact, that I just kept going *pfsss! pfsss!*... I always go *pfsss! pfsss!* when I'm enjoying myself... You know... When something's really wonderful... (*Illustrating.*) *Pfsss! pfsss!*... Well, for some reason everyone thought I was hissing the actors! Can you imagine? And they all began yelling: "Throw him out!... Get him out of here!..." So they did. They threw me out... They said I was trying to start a riot... The idiots!... That's justice for you!... "Just you wait," I told them. "I'll complain... I'll complain..."

And I did, let me tell you!... Next day I'm in one of your big department stores, and I see a door with a sign on it: COMPLAINT DEPARTMENT... "Just what I'm looking for," I tell myself. And I go inside.

Well, there's this crabby old gent sitting at a desk... An idiot, believe me!... And he asks me what's my complaint. So I get it off my chest. I tell him that I'm coming to complain that I was kicked out of the theater the day before just because I went *pfsss! pfsss!*... And he says: "So? What makes you think I give a good goddamn!"... Really!... And he calls me a "buffoon"!... Me, a buffoon!... Can you imagine?... I ask you, is that an idiot or isn't it?... Or blind maybe, one or the other... I mean, do I look like an ape? I may not be the handsomest thing on two feet, but a buffoon? Really!... Or maybe they hire idiots like that on purpose so they'll never understand what you're complaining about!... Talk about your soft jobs! Really!...

And if you think that was the end of it! Not on your life!... Yesterday I decided to take a little jaunt over the border for a change... You know, maybe buy a few things... Just over and back... Well, there I am with my packages, ready to come back across... But there's like a barrier right in the middle of the road, and a little house off to one side with a sign on it that says FRENCH CUSTOMS. A souvenir shop, I suppose... For the tourists... Anyway, like I say, there's this barrier... Now I ask you, why did they have to put it right in the middle of the road? It's not as if there wasn't plenty of room on the side, where it wouldn't be in the way... But no! The idiots!... Well, this character comes out of the little house all dressed up like some local gendarme or other... For the tourists, I suppose... And he asks me if I haven't got something to declare... "Declare? Me?" I answer... "Come now, monsieur," he tells me, and he gives me a look... "I'm sure you do..." "About what? About who?" I ask him... What does he take me for? Some kind of a stool-pigeon?... "About your duty," he tells me. "Because it's my job here to make sure no one dodges their duty..." "Damn right, my duty!" I tell him. "Damn right I've got something to declare!" "Aha!" he goes, "I thought so!" And he takes out his notebook... I look him straight in the eye and give him a little tap... "It's my duty to declare that I've had it up to here with damn halfwits and idiots!..." Well, I guess he thought it was him I was talking about, because next thing I know he's handing me a summons and telling me I'm charged with insulting an officer of the law, physical assault, and public obscenity, and that he'll see me in court!... And that I'm goddamn lucky he's not arresting me for smuggling!... Can you believe it?... I tried to explain... About the theater and all that... But he wouldn't even listen. "You can tell it to the bench," he tells me... So I look around, but damned if I can even find one...

Anyway, you can bet how disgusted I was after that! Especially me, with my principles, I mean... Because, if there's one thing I've got it's a sense of fair play... Of justice... Cool, even-handed justice... Cool, calm, collected... Never ruffled! Not like some people... All fluster and bluster, hustle and bustle... Hot today, cold tomorrow...

No... Unruffled, that's me... I save my ruffles for my shirtfronts! (*He chuckles.*) No flustle, no buster... (*Correcting himself.*) No fuster, no blustle... That is... (*With a shrug.*) Because what good is justice if it isn't fair, I ask you!... It's got to be fair... Very... Not just fairly... If not, it's just so much meaningless fluff... Fluff and piffle... (*About to correct himself.*) Pluff and... Fliff and... No, like I say, it's got to be... Really... If not, well... (*With a gesture.*) Pfff!

For example, if you want an idea how fair and square I am... Back a while I used to write reviews for the local paper... The racetrack turf sheet... Theater reviews... Maybe you read some... Well, every time I had one to write I'd make it a point never to go see the play. That way nobody could say I was prejudiced... See what I mean? You've got to be fair... Not let yourself be influenced... Besides, even when I decided to tear a play to pieces they could always get me to change my mind. Next day I'd publish a rave just to prove that the paper was completely neutral. Talk about being fair and impartial...

You see, when it comes to justice the first thing is equality. Everyone in society should be absolutely equal... I could never see why, just because somebody is better than me, they should think they can treat me the way... the way I treat my servant!... And I can't see why it's only the rich who should have money either... It's stupid! It doesn't make sense!... I mean, if they're rich that should be good enough for them!... They should give all their money to the poor... The ones who need it... In fact, I wrote an article about that once. Maybe you read it... I said poor people should be allowed to take whatever they want from anyone who's got more than they do... Well, you think they appreciated it?... Ha! Let me tell you!... Next day, some dirty tramp breaks into my flat and takes everything in sight!... That's the appreciation I got!... Anyway, he got his, believe me! I had him arrested and locked up, that scum!

You try to be nice to people and that's the thanks you get! I'm telling you... Goodness and virtue? Morality? Forget it!... Generosity?... Ha!... Why, can you imagine? There are people here in Paris who even sell it!... That's right!... I remember, last year... Around Carnival time... I'm passing by a shop with costumes and things in the window. And I see this sign: FAVORS FOR SALE. And underneath it says: BUY YOUR FAVORS HERE... LARGEST SELECTION, BEST PRICES IN PARIS... Or something like that... Now I ask you! If you have to pay for a favor it's not a favor, is it?... If you told anyone they'd never believe you!... Next they'll be selling kindness, and sympathy, and... (*Shaking his head.*) God! What a country!... If this keeps up we're done for, I'm telling you!

Besides, a country that doesn't have a strong sense of justice... Why, just the other day... Maybe you read about it... They sentenced some poor guy to death... And what for?... Because he went and cut some little kid to pieces... Yes, that's what I said... Sentenced him to death... And that's your justice?... Why, years ago didn't Solomon try to do exactly the same thing?... Cut some baby in half... Remember?... And everyone will tell you he was a great king! Go figure it out!... Not like you and me... How many of us can be kings when we want to go cut some kid to pieces?... I ask you... Justice?...

But just try telling that to the courts and see how far you get!... Ha!... Don't make me laugh! The courts... It's the courts we should get rid of if it's justice you're after!... You hear what I'm saying?... Because the more courts, the more criminals, believe me!... That's right... Just think about it... If we didn't have courts we wouldn't need any criminals to keep them in business!... You know what I mean?... (*He exits, shaking his head.*)

Georges Feydeau, *L'Homme intègre*

The Lawyers and the Lady
or
All's Fair in Love and Law

My hero's name was Jacques.

He was a roofer by trade, a Belgian by birth, and none too bright in general.

Each year his wife would present him with a set of triplets.

One assumed the cause merely to be some odd talent on her part. (None too flattering for Jacques, who, at any rate, never spoke of it.)

One day, however, he lost his wife and, soon after, took another.

The next year the second duplicated the first's accomplishment.

The public, of course, reacted.

Jacques was finally acknowledged as a worthy collaborator in the event.

Pleased with the long-due admiration for his prowess, he was amply repaid for his earlier unwarranted disregard.

Brussels was justly proud of her citizen.

He was mentioned in the foreigners' guides to the city as a tourist attraction.

A public treasure, he was cherished by one and all.

In short, he enjoyed a most agreeable notoriety throughout the city.

One evening, at the tavern, he offered to see home one of the more besotted of his friends, deeply into his cups.

As they walked along the canal the drunkard turned to him and said: "My wife is doing me dirt… You, you have eighteen children, and you're a good sort… Here's my money and my watch. They're yours. I will them to you…"

And he jumped into the canal.

It all happened so fast that Jacques had no time to find a notary to witness the transaction.

Now, if you found a man's body in a canal and his watch in his friend's pocket, I'm sure you would be the first to make unpleasant suppositions as to how said friend had come into possession of said watch.

So I ask you to put yourself in the place of Belgian justice, quite new at the time and eager for something to do. (It was 1831, and Belgium, you see, had just been invented.)

In brief, Jacques was arrested.

He was, of course, innocent as could be.

Sympathy and public outrage mounted, and the gates of the prison were about to be flung wide, when an elder reactionary pronounced these words, later to become proverbial:

"Haste makes waste."

And so Jacques was kept in prison, thus simply deferring—or

so it seemed—his ultimate triumph and glorious acquittal.

From the depths of his cell our roofer held sway over the hearts of the populace with a pity it usually reserves these days for well-diggers buried alive in their wells.

Each member of the court was asked in turn: "When will you let our dear Jacques go free?"

To which the answer was always: "Any day... Just a few formalities..."

The whole city would happily have furnished their hero's bail. But "Why bother," they thought each day, "since he's going to be freed tomorrow!"

Besides, it gave them all an excellent reason to rail against justice's injustices... So to speak... The inequities of a detention that wrenched a father from his family, a workman from his trade...

Thus by day they might send round a braised loin of veal for his children to eat and mattresses for them to sleep on.

By night they might clamber up onto the rooftops—their neighbors', of course—and furtively rip off tiles here and there so that, once free, our good roofer would have no dearth of employment.

At length the day of the trial arrived.

The night before, the presiding judge—a kindly old gent, Dutilbag by name—had gone down to Jacques's cell to tell him:

"It's tomorrow, at eleven in the morning, monsieur. Send word to your family to come fetch you at the court. By noon it will all be over and done with, and you will be a free man."

Then he had added, purely out of habit:

"Unless, that is, there's some reason to detain you."

Next morning, a compassionate crowd had invaded the tribunal.

The prisoner appeared between two gendarmes... Gendarmes? Rather mother hens, let me call them, so devoted were they and concerned for their charge's welfare.

Jacques himself was so certain of his impending freedom that he had brought to the trial his few modest possessions, wrapped up in a checkered kerchief.

As his unusual family looked on, smothered by the crowd's affection, he gestured fondly in their direction, as if to say: "Go home and put the goose on the fire. I'll join you in a moment."

And so they did.

The spectators, the other magistrates, the jurors... One and all were champing at the bit with impatience.

But the kindly old presiding judge, in an effort to calm them, observed:

"Procedure, good people... Procedure!... Your Jacques will be set free, but for heaven's sake let us observe the proper procedure!"

Now, the defendant's innocence was such a foregone conclusion that no one had even thought to provide him with counsel. As it happened, however, the judge noticed, sitting there in the crowd, the practitioner *par excellence* of the Brussels bar, the barrister Van der

Linden. With a glance and a nod he invited him to come and assume Jacques's defense.

★

The celebrated orator replied with a shrug of the shoulders, as if to protest:

"Why bother? The truth is so obvious it will speak for itself."

His Honor gave a second entreating glance and nod that seemed to say:

"Procedure, my friend... Procedure!"

The barrister was, in fact, rather suffocating in the midst of the multitude; and, deciding that he would doubtless be more comfortable at the bench, approached, took his place, and prepared to plead for the defense, albeit needlessly, of course.

The spectators applauded with delight that colossus of eloquence, who was about to defend innocence with the power of his oratory.

And at length it began.

★

The witnesses, ready to testify on Jacques's behalf, would all have spoken up at once, with one voice, had the judge, pointing, not silenced them abruptly:

"Please, messieurs... Be seated!"

In their box, the jurors were fidgeting with impatience, eager to dispose of the case without ado.

"Procedure, my friends... Procedure!" he muttered in their direction.

★

Finally, the barrister Van der Linden rose to his feet.

A sublime and worshipful silence came over the crowd, ready to imbibe his every precious word.

And, from the depths of his immense talent, our Belgian Demosthenes summoned up this deathless assertion:

"I rest my case, Your Honor!"

The sentence was punctuated with a thunder of applause that brought chips of plaster raining down from the ceiling.

Then came the government's turn to state its case.

The prosecutor for the Crown, a certain barrister Van Brower, was a talented young man, to be sure. Only newly admitted to the bar, however, he was about to undergo his baptism of fire, as it were, in the present proceedings.

Foreseeing the outcome, he had whispered to the bailiff, a moment before his adversary's brilliant impromptu plea:

"Have them bring my coach round to the rear, if you please."

And he had gathered up all his papers in view of a hasty exit.

There he stood, concealing in his robe's long sleeves his hands already gloved for his departure.

He had, of course, quite simply decided to withdraw the accusation.

But just as he was parting his lips to speak...

Just then, suddenly, the swish of silks rustled through the air.

Mademoiselle Cécile Dutilbag, the presiding judge's daughter, was entering the courtroom.

Said Cécile Dutilbag was a beautiful young thing.

The wealthiest of gentlemen had sought her hand in marriage.

Pitiless, mademoiselle had rejected them all.

Her most recent rebuff had, in fact, caused something of a scandal, disdaining, as she did, the prospect of becoming the wife of the gilt-tongued barrister Van der Linden.

But her heart at last had spoken, conferring its favor on none other than the Crown's young prosecutor, our barrister Van Brower, to whom, indeed, she had plighted her troth the very night before.

Much in love and beloved, as she knew herself to be, she had come to witness for herself the maiden victory of her betrothed.

Jacques, meanwhile—overcome by the heat—was sitting fast asleep, oblivious to her entrance and, indeed, to everything else.

The prosecutor, at the sight of his inamorata—whose tender glance seemed lovingly to say: "Be victorious, my love!"—felt a twinge of anger toward the accused.

"Damned Jacques!" he thought. "Why must he be the one? With some *bona fide* scoundrel I could have caused an utter sensation!"

Slowly he removed his gloves.

Before his beloved angel had appeared, he had decided to withdraw the accusation. Now, still holding to that resolve, he felt he must at least adorn his withdrawal with a few choice flowers of rhetoric. He was, in a word, eloquent.

"Here, here!" the lovely Cécile's smile seemed to tell him.

"Bravo, my son!" concurred the judge with an approving glance.

Ambition, as they say, feeds on success. The more we get, the more we want.

Our young barrister decided to be not only eloquent, but scrupulously attentive to judicial procedure as well.

And so he proceeded to invoke the observation that appearances can be deceiving, and to prove, with consummate perspicacity and skill, that such, indeed, might well be the case, even with the likes of the much loved Monsieur Jacques.

"Here, here!" his charming betrothed's gracious smile kept urging.

"Bravo, my son!" murmured the judge again, under his breath.

Barrister Van Brower had, indeed, begun warming—nay, heating—to his task. But just as he was, adroitly, about to come round to his inevitable withdrawal, he was fiercely interrupted by the prisoner's celebrated defender.

Before, when Cécile had made her entrance, the latter, as you might well expect, had suffered a silent fit of jealous pique.

"Ah, my sweet!" he had muttered to himself. "So! You think you're going to watch him carry the day, do you? This hero of yours... This novice that you preferred to me!... Well, we'll see! I'll show you that you chose the chaff instead of the wheat!"

And he lay in wait, listening to his rival's every word, on the watch for the slightest flaw, the merest chink in his argument, ready to swoop without mercy and plunge in like a wedge of steel.

The awaited occasion presented itself, and back strode the voluble Van der Linden into the lists with withering harangue.

The spectators, unaware that the scene had changed, assumed that the first act of the drama, as it were, was simply continuing, and they broke into wild applause.

The judge, fearing in this ovation a prejudice in his future son-in-law's disfavor, reprimanded them severely.

Then he called the barrister too to order.

All of which noticeably changed the atmosphere of the proceedings.

Impassioned, our Demosthenes objected:

"First the Court abused the good faith of the defense, and now it would attempt to impede it in its proper exercise!"

And at every turn he went smashing juridically through the prosecutor's charges, like a bull in a china shop.

Several of his impressive oratorical devices even attracted the fair Cécile's attention.

For a moment she almost appeared to be reconsidering…

"No matter," mused barrister Van Brower, love-crazed and jealous. "I'll thrash him all the same."

And he hammered away at those "deceiving appearances" that he had earlier invoked, citing each one, in turn, and drawing from them conclusions at once lucid, precise, and incriminating.

The judge nodded his sage approval.

The spectators, always convinced by whoever speaks last, felt their convictions shaken and their confidence in Jacques undone.

The jurors shook their heads in surprise and murmured: "But... But... We never knew... No one told us..."

And on and on and on held forth the prosecutor for the Crown.

He dredged up Naked Truth from her well, so naked that not a single spectator could keep from exclaiming: "Good grief, but that Jacques is a scoundrel! A wretch! A swine!..."

Needless to day, the illustrious Van der Linden rose, in turn, to refute every claim.

But alas, too late. The damage had been done.

The jurors had seen the light.

"He must be daft," they said to themselves.

"Does he know what he's doing?"

"He can't make up his mind. First he says he rests his case, then he turns around and pleads it."

"Is he just being pigheaded?"

Et cetera, et cetera...

The judge, at length, was obliged to conclude the deliberations.

Father-in-law and magistrate, he proved instinctively to be more the former than the latter.

In a show of approval for his daughter's good taste, he pronounced summarily for his son-in-law-to-be.

The jurors trampled one another in their race to the jury room, eager to concur in His Honor's learned verdict.

As for Jacques, he woke up to the joyful huzzas of the Belgian citizenry, now finally enlightened, hailing his lengthy sentence to prison at hard labor.

When the crowd had dispersed, I heard a philosopher, who had attended the proceedings off in a corner, muttering, as he left, two lines no doubt inspired by Propertius:

"I used to wonder—but, alas, no more—
How 'twas a lass that caused the Trojan War."

Eugène Chavette, *Deux vers de Properce*

The Volatile Mother-in-Law
or
Science to the Rescue

Far be it from me to deprive you, in particular, or Humanity, in general, of the following curious communication sent to me by one of my readers, a member of the Academy of Sciences and one of the most distinguished chemists in all of France. Permit me...

(*Reading.*)

"Dear Colleague,

"I must say I was struck by one of your recent articles; the one in which you made mention of that unfortunate mother-in-law frightened to death by the terrifying spectacle of a stuffed lion's head suddenly bursting forth in a roar and darting fire from its eyes.

"Myself, I was able, some twenty years ago—well beyond the statute of limitations, I hasten to add—to dispose of my own equally unfortunate mother-in-law by a process which, while requiring some rudimentary scientific ability, is nonetheless worthy of the most serious consideration.

"Allow me to take advantage of your widely-read and informative column to give the details. I daresay a number of your readers— the married gentlemen, at least—may find them quite worthwhile.

"After only a few months of marriage, I had already begun to experience a passionate loathing of my mother-in-law; the kind that, even in the gentlest of creatures, as lamb-like as myself, fill the heart to overflowing with a torrential eruption of the most savage instincts.

"Why not kill her, you ask? Oh, believe me, I had every

intention! But the question was how!

"Much though I admire our national *gendarmerie*, I always do my utmost to avoid the opportunity of confronting the courageous minions of the law who do honor to that institution.

"Now then, even the least little murder, no matter whose—mothers-in-law included—is certain to produce a knock at the door from one of their conscientious number, of greater or lesser rank.

"I had, therefore, to devise a means of dispatching the old lady without raising the merest scintilla of indiscreet suspicion, and one that would withstand the scrutiny of the keenest of our human bloodhounds.

"Being a chemist, I quite naturally turned to chemistry for my solution...

"As luck would have it, during the summer, my mother-in-law was in the habit of dressing from head to toe entirely in cotton.

"Cotton was her passion!

"'Cotton... Cotton...' she never tired of droning. 'It's the healthiest thing for a body to wear!'

"I really don't remember just how the idea took shape in my brain, but one fine day... I still have to laugh every time I think about it... One fine day, with all the skill and stealth of a cat-burglar, I managed to make off with several articles of her wardrobe: stockings, underwear, skirt, blouse, and such.

"I took them to my laboratory and, by steeping them in a simple and well-known mixture of nitric and sulphuric acids, I transformed that array of harmless, peaceful cotton into a belligerent cellulose nitrate just waiting to explode.

"Then I saw to it, not without diabolical cunning, that my

mother-in-law would next put on that costume of utterly volatile potential.

"The sun, that day, was unmercifully hot...

"She was sitting on a stone bench, reading some example of inept contemporary literature.

"Not far off, I had resolutely taken up my post, armed with a powerful magnifying glass, and focusing an intense beam of light on the poor woman's clothing.

"It didn't take long. A scream, a spectacular flash... And that was that!

"The medical examiner concluded that my mother-in-law had been an inveterate alcoholic, and refused to consider the accident as anything but a rare case of spontaneous human combustion.

"I saw no reason to disagree with an expert.

Yours truly... Etc. etc."

Just imagine! If not for the statute of limitations...

Alphonse Allais, *Scientia liberatrix, ou La Belle-mère explosible*

Widow's Pique
or
After the Fall

At two hundred fifty-six rue Rougemont, third floor front, in a posh apartment—high rent, taxes not included—there lived a family by the name of Martin.

It numbered three: a father, a mother, a son... One of each.

Now, the father, just before my little tale begins, had retired from the insurance profession.

Founder and director of a firm that insured against lawyerly skulduggery, his clients were legion and he had amassed a huge fortune.

A placid sort, but gruff and unsociable—quite the opposite of his wife and son—he heartily abhorred the whole social whirl, with its *fêtes*, its balls, its theater galas, and the like.

His wife and son, unmindful of spousal and filial respect—respectively—considered him, in a word, a boor.

As for madame, she hovered delicately and gracefully betwixt thirty and forty summers.

Pretty, *chic*, and flighty, she looked for all the world like her husband's daughter and her son's elder sister.

Said son, a nice little ne'er-do-well of eighteen, and spoiled utterly beyond belief by his *maman*, had already taken to borrowing rather substantial sums of money from friends of his father, sundry of his purveyors, and even, once, from the concierge.

But a mother's heart is a veritable wagonload of indulgence; madame would pay the young man's debts, and monsieur was never the wiser.

Until one day, that is, when the junior Martin committed a mischievous indiscretion of such scandalous proportion that it was quite impossible to conceal it from his father.

Monsieur, summarily, got up on his high horse—nay, his highest of chargers—raged, ranted, and raved, and decided that Gaston would enlist forthwith and serve five years in the army.

But mother's eyes are boundless, endless reservoirs of tears: madame was quick to loose the sluice, and wept a torrent.

In vain: obdurate, the senior Martin would not be moved.

The only concession he was willing to accord the *mater lachrymosa* was to allow her to accompany her offspring to the barracks gate.

Which she did.

When the moment came to wrench herself away, the sentry sergeant, touched by her sobs, suggested that madame go put in a good word for her son, in person, with the captain and the colonel.

Disconsolate, she complied, beginning with the captain, a thirty-year-young Romeo at the ready.

She remained for a quarter of an hour and left somewhat consoled.

Then it was the colonel's turn.

Indeed, the colonel, pushing sixty—pulling it, rather—took longer.

Madame's visit lasted almost three-quarters of an hour.

But at length she left, consoled quite completely.

33

Not for long, however, because Gaston's first letters were disturbing in the extreme.

To begin with, someone had eaten all his chocolate.

Then followed the whole distressing litany of army-life woes: hard bed, vile food, distasteful chores, backbreaking drills, despicable comrades, malicious pranks, teasing, bullying… Et cetera, et cetera…

Finally, one day, Madame Martin had had more than she could bear.

She took the train and arrived at the colonel's quarters.

The colonel hadn't aged but he hadn't got any younger-looking either.

At the end of three agonizing quarter-hours of lament, relenting, he threw down his arms, threw up his hands, and, breaking every rule, granted private Martin a one-week leave.

Next evening, father, mother, and son, reunited, were dining *en famille*.

Monsieur was a trifle less his obdurate self for the occasion.

High time, I might add…

After the meal, as was his long-standing custom, he stood at the balcony, elbows on the rail, leaned out, and lit up his pipe. His trusty meerschaum…

Mother and son, meanwhile, were in the sitting-room, chatting. "So," madame was saying, "you tell me there's no possible way out of that awful regiment?"

"None," replied Gaston. Unless I got myself discharged for physical reasons… Or if I happened to become a widow's only son…"

"A widow's only son, you say?"

"Quite, *maman*. A widow…"

Madame pondered for a moment, then suddenly asked:

"Are you particularly fond of your father?"

"Not at all, *maman*. Are you?"

"Me?… Pfff!"

A gesture of disdain toward the gentleman in question accompanied her exclamation. And she went on:

"Just watch…"

At that moment Monsieur Martin was leaning rather far forward.

His center of gravity was not exactly beyond the rail, but it wasn't far from it.

It was obvious that an ever so slight displacement of his mass, in the direction of the street below, would result, first, in a somersault, then in a subsequent rapid descent.

With catlike tread, Madame Martin tiptoed up behind her spouse, grasped the seat of his trousers in both hands, and—poof!—sent him head over heels, by the most expeditious route, to join the object he had been contemplating so intently on the sidewalk.

The move was executed with an energy and dispatch that one would scarcely have expected to find in a woman of such cultivated appearance.

As for monsieur, the pavement broke his fall.

And the fall broke his neck.

And, alas, his meerschaum. The latter, with a sharp little "plick" of snapping clay; the former, with a "splonk," the dull, ponderous thud of a side of beef hitting asphalt.

A young woman just coming from the theatre had her dress quite splattered. As she began to wipe off a number of grayish splotches with her kerchief a considerate passer-by assured her: "Really, madame, you needn't. It's only brain, it doesn't soil. Let it dry, and tomorrow, with a good brushing, it won't even show."

(Incidentally, he was misinformed: the human brain is a very fatty substance—phosphoric, if I'm not mistaken—and it stains as much as any other. But be that as it may...)

In the meantime madame and her son came hurtling down the stairs.

"Gustave! Poor, dear Gustave!" yowled the wife.

"Papa! Poor, dear papa!" howled the son.

And the crowd of bystanders, moved to compassion by their awesome and twofold woe, doffed their hats in respect.

A big, fat doctor came running over, huffing and puffing. He pronounced monsieur officially dead, then took their name and address so as to send his bill in the morning for the minor inconvenience.

Monsieur's funeral, as funerals go, was as nice as it could be.

In uniform and black crepe armband, young Gaston, convulsed with sobs, led the mourners.

"Poor child," murmured the crowd.

The brief inquest that ensued determined that, indeed, monsieur's demise had been occasioned by a fall brought on by an attack of apoplexy.

Gaston, as only son of a widow, returned to civilian life, much to the disappointment of the colonel, who had become unusually taken with madame.

Now, my deep affection for widow and orphan notwithstanding, I'll not keep from you the fact that the mourning period was cut somewhat short.

Rather sooner than decorum might have led one to expect, they made their reemergence onto the social scene.

(There are those who would waltz, as it were, before the gates of Hades.)

But now comes the drollest part of my whole tale: Madame Martin, with her son's consent and blessing, is about to get married again.

To the colonel.

It hasn't yet occurred to my frivolous friends that Gaston, by said union, will cease to be a widow's only son, and will be recalled straightway to his regiment.

As you might imagine, I've been quite careful not to alert them to this detail.

And I anticipate with pleasure the look on poor Gaston's face.

Alphonse Allais, *Fils de veuve*

Cream and Punishment
(Translated from the Russian)

It was, I believe, the surpassing ugliness of the old woman that attracted me to her.

When, on my amble through a side street of her wretched slum, I caught sight of the disgusting creature at her window—with her pallid, purplescent visage, her beady eyes agleam with lubricity and lust, her frizzed brown wig, so obviously artificial—there welled up within my brain a gust of that fetid concupiscence that will, from time to time, haunt the fantasies of certain callow young men and reprehensible old lechers.

Close to, the old woman was abhorrent beyond all telling.

The purplish blotches of her aged, sagging jowls were made all the more repugnant by a rice-powder film of debatable hue, acquired, I imagine, from some beldame herbalist of ill repute, an abortionist more than likely.

Repeated repairs to her enormous denture had placed teeth of a dubious murky blue side by side with others of what looked like ancient ivory.

And if, at that moment, my mind had not been thoroughly lucid and composed, I should doubtless have thought myself the plaything of some agonizing and woeful nightmare.

Surely it was not necessity that drove her to engage in her loathsome calling, for everything in her lodging bespoke a life, indeed, of almost prosperous comfort.

Fine white sheets decked out her bed, a bed worthy of tidily well-to-do village burghers. An antique provincial chest of massive oak stood solidly in a corner, with that rich air, that air—unexplainable by any logic—of being abundantly filled; that air that let *those of my kind* distinguish without fail, and at a glance, the full chests from the empty.

She gazed in lustful admiration at the chocolate-cream trifle I was holding, and into which I had, at that moment, just bitten.

"Your trifle looks delicious," she cackled in a vulgar harpy's voice that she attempted to render warblingly suggestive.

It was, in fact, a trifle of uncommonly exquisite taste, presented to me only shortly before by my fellow countryman, Ivan Irksomitch, the most fashionable confectioner in the city. A chocolate-cream trifle too delectable for words...

I took perverse delight, however, in contradicting the old woman.

"My trifle?" sneered I. "It's vile... Foul... Distasteful beyond belief!... I found it this morning on Montmartre, in the swillpot of a sordid bistro."

"Nasty wag!" she brayed.

In the course of the conversation that ensued, in much the same tenor, the idea struck me—at first the merest of vague suggestions—to kill this harridan *over a trifle!*

And I pronounced these words, muttered under my breath: "over a trifle... over a trifle..."

From that moment on I was seized with the irresistible urge—the obsession—to murder the old woman.

★

My blade was one of that hinged variety commonly called a "jackknife," named for its inventor, a Britisher, one Jack B. Nimble. (Some attribute it to his compatriot, Jack B. Quick, but no matter...) It was quite the instrument ideally suited to my purpose. Sharp-pointed blade, handle comfortable to the fist, and a thick metal ring pushed into place about the hinge to keep it from closing inopportunely...

All at once the old hag turned her back. Then and there I struck my blow, hard and true, plunging my blade to the hilt... Well placed, I recall...

As the odious old crone went crumbling to her knees in a pose of utter desperation, I held the knife firmly, pressing tight the metal ring against the wound to prevent the blood from escaping.

When, at length, she had croaked her last rasping "aaargh"; when the hemorrhage within had snuffed out her miserable life, I removed the horde of gold coins and other valuables from a drawer in the massive oaken chest, and, closing the door behind me, quickly took my leave.

The entire scene had lasted not a scant ten minutes. With no noise, no blood...

I betook myself toward the home of my mistress, a young lady by the name of Nini, and whom my friends have affectionately dubbed Nini Novgorod ever since I became her lover.

As I walked, a pair of officers of the law approached slowly in my direction.

Why I cannot say, but their placid demeanor sent an icy shiver fluttering through me. They seemed singularly calm... Indeed, too calm...

Then, as I fixed my haggard, wild-eyed gaze, with brazen abandon, squarely upon theirs, each, with an almost mechanical gesture as they passed close by my side, raised his hand to his cap.

By and by, other gendarmes along my path, glared at in like manner, saluted me as well, confirming my *idée fixe*.

"So little do we take you for an assassin, monsieur," they seemed to be saying, "that we have no hesitation in greeting you with respect."

★

Nini Novgorod was not at home. Automatically, I cast my glance at the mirror in her salon... Suddenly there I stood, convulsed with what was perhaps the most jubilant peal of laughter my body has ever known.

All at once I understood my unaccustomed prestige before the minions of the law.

My knife, apparently, despite the metal ring, had not sealed the old woman's wound completely.

A trickle of blood had somehow seeped through.

It had found its way to my frock coat's left lapel and had spread into the shape of a little red rosette.

A hero's decoration, with ribbon and all!

Yes, they had thought it was the Légion d'honneur, the bloody idiots!

Alphonse Allais, *Crime russe*

Disorder in the Court

There was once a young lawyer who was down on his luck. He had never had a client. Of course, he wasn't the only one. But still, that wasn't much consolation.

Now, it's only fair to explain that, if he hadn't had a case yet, it's because he was waiting for one of those really big ones. Something sensational... Not just any ordinary, run-of-the-mill affair, but the kind that gives you an instant reputation and makes you a celebrity. The problem is that, to get one like that, you've got to be famous first. It's a rather vicious circle.

Well, after a lot of very serious thought, he had come to the conclusion that the only way was to know a criminal. But, unfortunately, you don't run into first-rate criminals every day of the week. Especially ones who take you into their confidence... "No," he pondered, "good luck doesn't happen. You've got to go out and make it!" And so he thought of all the people he knew, trying to find one with an innate bent for crime, someone he could easily get to commit one, and then plead the case. Not quite cricket, perhaps... But then, he had absolute faith in his ability. "What's the harm?" he kept telling himself. "I'm sure to get him off!..." Which was enough to salve his less-than-demanding conscience...

The criminal-to-be that he finally selected was a certain young woman, the mistress of a friend, and one that he knew had a vicious, jealous temper. At least, judging by things he had always heard her say... Like: "Just let me catch him cheating!... You'll see! I'll poke her eyes out!... Both of them!... With a hatpin!..." No need to explain that the "her" referred to was any potential rival whatsoever...

At any rate, our hero took care, subtly, to fan the flame. And in time, when the vixen seemed appropriately primed and ready for the kill, he casually announced that her lover was getting married.

The results of this blatant falsehood were three in number. One after another, and in rapid succession. First, she flew into a blind, uncontrollable rage, smashing everything in the young man's apartment she could lay her hands on. Then, coming to her senses, she boxed his ears with a pair of well-aimed punches that could de-horn the head of the staunchest of cuckolds. After which she turned sharply on her heels and made a beeline for her lover's, intent on giving him a proper piece of her mind, as well as a number of holes in the belly with a knife that she knew he kept conveniently on his desk.

As luck would have it, the knife in question was a cheap wooden letter-opener. Not terribly lethal... When the young woman leapt, headlong, to plunge it into the traitor's heart, it hit against a billfold, providentially placed, and broke harmlessly in two.

The victim's concierge, however—sensing impending drama—had thought it best to investigate. Leaping upstairs four steps at a time, he arrived to witness the grotesque attack. With undaunted courage—and once he saw that there wasn't the slightest danger—he collared the would-be assassin and dragged her to the police, screaming and in tears, protests of a baffled lover notwithstanding.

Immediately the wheels of Justice began to turn. True, our lawyer, whom the prisoner had chosen—as planned—would surely have preferred a more substantial crime, never doubting his ultimate, resounding victory. Still, all things considered, he was really quite ecstatic. The newspapers were full of the curious affair, shrouded as it was in mystery. And all the more intriguing since the murderess had done nothing, from the moment of her arrest, but bawl her eyes out and burst into fits of the wildest hysterics...

The day finally arrived for the jury to hear the testimony. Frankly, they didn't understand much of the lover's story. Even less of the concierge's. And as for the defendant, they couldn't even begin to guess... She just sat there cursing everybody. Her lover, especially... Which didn't do a lot, in the long run, to help her case... But at last the young lawyer rose confidently to his feet. He cleared his throat... He paused... He looked at the jury... Then he started to talk...

And he talked... And he talked... So much that nobody could make head or tail... Hours later, when the smoke had cleared and the jury had deliberated, his client had been sentenced to ten years at hard labor. And the concierge, to death, if that matters to anybody...

What's more, when the lover learned what his friend had been up to, he challenged him to a duel. A ripping good time, too... But not for the lawyer, who got his just deserts. And not with a cheap wooden letter-opener, either...

To add insult, as it were, to injury, our ambitious young friend—dismayed, disgraced, and now distinctly disfigured—was dispassionately disbarred.

Talk about luck...

Léon Xanrof, *Pas de chance*

Bag and Baggage

It's a few years already since it happened.

My friend Jojo and me, we got the tip from this old traveling salesman... Sold baskets and things... Seems he was going around one day, out in the sticks, and he noticed this house in the middle of nowhere. An old widow lives there, they tell him. A little soft in the head. All by herself, no maid, no nothing... And never goes out, not even to shop. The grocers and people bring her things. Butter, eggs, whatever... Don't even go in the house. Just leave their stuff on a bench outside and pick up the money she puts out for them.

Now Jojo, he tells me that, since we both heard about it the same time, we should do the job together, just the two of us. No need to let no one else get in on it... So he gives me a few francs and I go and buy us a second-hand truck. Just big enough but not too big... And I go outside and get some dead branches and rocks, stuff like that, and put it all in so's to give it some weight. Because I figure that later, if things go bad, and if they know it was empty when we took it out there, that would give them a pretty good clue, if you see what I mean.

Afterwards, we decide, I'll take the trunk with me to Paris. Better than just leaving it there in her house, or outside somewhere. Easy enough just to close the place up and let them think she's gone away. On a trip or something. The less hullabaloo the better... Besides, in Paris, no problem. Me and Jojo, we got this friend who'll take care of it for us. Burn it up, he tells us...

When we get to the old bag's place it's almost dark. We tell her we got some samples of wine to show her. Question is, will she fall for it? Will she let us come in, seeing as how she doesn't exactly like strangers.

But she does… Hook, line, and sinker. And when we get inside… Well, it's over before you know it. Believe me, I seen Jojo at work plenty of times before, but never that good. And fast? In no time he's got her by the neck, and he's throwing her down on the sofa, like you'd think she's light as a feather, I'm telling you. Hunchback or not, he's all muscle, that one! Not too much upstairs maybe… When it comes to the thinking part, the do's and don't's… Well, that's my department. He's the brawn, I'm the brain. Lucky thing too, because between you and I I'm no good for none of the heavy stuff. Not me. Fact is, I damn near puked just holding down her legs while Jojo was wringing her neck, like you'd think it was the easiest thing in the world for him…

Well, after a while she stops moving, and that's that. Funny how big her body looks. But we manage to get it in the trunk and push the cover down. A pretty tight fit, but that's good because that way it won't go bouncing around inside… Then, soon as the trunk is all locked up, we go looking through the furniture to see what she's got stashed away. First off, we find about eight hundred francs in her drawers. In gold… Then a handful of five-franc pieces she was hiding in a shoe, one of them fancy old-fashioned ones, and that fall out when we turn it upside down. Of all the crazy places… And a bunch of medals and jewels in a teapot, and papers with the name of some bank in funny letters that we can't make heads or tails out of because they're all in English. But we take them anyway because maybe… You never know…

Funny, but with all that work, all that poking around and sticking our noses here and there, turning the place inside out, we didn't hardly have time to think "What's next?" Fact is, when we lugged the trunk to the station and filled out the paper for it, I didn't even give a thought what there was inside. Anyhow, we figured the train was the best way to get it to Paris, what with my chum Jacquot, who's a baggage inspector there, and I knew he wouldn't give me no trouble, or make me open it up or anything… So we shake hands at the station, me and Jojo, and he takes the train in the other direction so's he can go say hello to his family as long as he's in the neighborhood. And he brings along this real nice doll he found in the old bag's house, porcelain or something, to give it to his little niece.

Now, fact is, when you're in a train a while without nothing to do except sit and think, your nerves got time to settle down and get back to normal. All of a sudden you're not feeling all brave like you were before. A little uneasy even... Meanwhile we're getting closer and closer to Paris, and I know we'll be getting to the station in no time. I feel like I just want to get up and stretch, and get out of that stuffy damn train. But it goes and stops under some bridge or other, and just stands there. And waits. Like you'd think it's going to stand there forever... Well, after a while it starts up again and we finally pull in.

While they're unloading all the baggage, all the trunks and things, and piling them into this big hall, I run out in the street to try and find a cab. But there's something important going on that day, some big horse race or other I think, and there's trains coming in from everywhere. And all the cabs that hang around in front of the station, they're all grabbed up, every damn one. So I got to go run a couple dozen blocks just to find one that's free. Well, I finally get back to the station, and by now almost all the bags and trunks and packages are gone. There's maybe only seven or eight things left on that big counter they use for the inspection. And there's mine, sitting between this wooden mannequin and a bundle of underwear.

First thing, I look around for my friend. I figure he's got to be there somewhere, my chum Jacquot... I ask one of the other guys working there where he is, and he tells me Jacquot is sick, and he hasn't been to work for two whole days now. So I ask him to come over and mark my trunk so's I can take it out. But just then, just when I'm going over to it, and him right behind me with a piece of chalk in his hand, I see this chief inspector with three stripes on his cap on the other side of the counter. And he's crabbing and griping like you'd think the world was coming to an end, because he just had some kind of a run-in with one of them society ladies over some package of hers or other.

Me, I'm standing there with my hand on my trunk. Then the inspector, he starts growling at me, if I got anything to declare. And I don't even have time to answer. Already he's telling me to open it up. That's when I get this funny feeling on the back of my neck, like you'd think the skin was crawling or something. And I'm telling you, my

48

arms are shaking in my sleeves, and... And I start tapping my pockets and feeling around like I'm looking for my keys... Like I really want to find them! But in no time this other guy is standing there with a bunch of skeleton keys... I take a look over at the exit. There's inspectors everywhere, and two of them at the door, one on each side...

The guy is already trying out his keys to see which one'll fit. And me, I'm in a daze. I see them all standing there but I don't know where I am. My mind's a blank... Finally one of the keys goes in... It works. It turns... The cover pops open...

And all of a sudden I'm laughing like an idiot! There, in the trunk... What's in there but all kinds of clothes and things! Kids' sweaters, and shoes, and collars, and bars of soap... I'm telling you... And while they're poking around inside, me, I'm thinking about the poor fool galloping somewhere in Paris, behind a cabby who's got a crazy old bag's body packed up on the seat beside him! And the best part? Fact is, I never even heard a word about it after that. Maybe whoever took it was afraid to talk and get himself in trouble. Who knows? All I know is I have a good laugh every time I think of his face when he opened my trunk!... By the way, I found this nice woolen vest in his. I been wearing it every winter for the last three years. It keeps me good and warm...

Tristan Bernard, *La Visite des bagages*

The Last Laugh

Don't ask me to tell you a funny story.

I won't.

I'd rather go on living, thank you. You too, I bet.

You start out telling a nice little story, and lots of times things don't end up the way you'd like.

For example, they ended up pretty bad for this friend of mine... No names... But I'm telling you, could he tell funny stories!

Funny? Like you wouldn't believe... Especially this one of his... But when I say "funny"... Because it's funny how there are some funny stories that aren't funny at all. Not "ha-ha" funny, if you know what I mean. But his was. "Ha-ha" funny, that is...

He worked on it for years to get it just right. Funny how hard he worked on his funny story... Some days all night... Then finally, voilà! Finished. Perfect. Not the least little flaw, not off by a hair... A hundred percent funny, every least little bit, believe me... Perfection itself. So funny, you'd think he invented the laugh, this friend of mine...

Because sure, there were lots of funny stories before, but they couldn't hold a candle. Not to my friend's. Not to his. But no names... I'd rather not...

Anyway, to make a long story short, one day he goes into this café where he always used to go. There's not a soul in the place.

Except the waitress, that is. And she's just standing around with her head in the clouds, or somewhere, filing her nails.

"What's up?" she asks him.

"Nothing," he answers.

And they yawn, the two of them.

"That's all you can tell me?"

"I guess so…"

Then he stops and thinks for a minute, and, just like that, he says:

"If you want, I can tell you a funny story."

"Oh yes," she squeals. "Please!" And she stands there clapping her hands.

So he does. He tells her his story. Actually, he had just added a hilarious new bit. A real clincher, if you know what I mean. Talk about genius. Believe me, you'll see… Anyway, he doesn't get two sentences out of his mouth, and "pow!", she gets smacked in the kisser with this line, funny like you wouldn't believe, and she's laughing herself sick. But that's not the end of it . My friend gears up, he picks up speed… Now she's in stitches. Absolute stitches…

"Enough!" she begs him, all doubled up. "Please!… Please, no more!" And she's holding her sides.

But my friend guns the motor, gives it the gas, and starts in with that extra new bit I was telling you… Damn! You should have seen her! Coming at her from all sides… Hearing him, watching him… His voice, his moves, his gestures… Because he was an actor too, my friend. I don't think I mentioned. Funny? Like you wouldn't…

Anyway, there she is, poor thing, gasping and gagging.

"Please! I give up!... I... I..."

But he couldn't care less. He just kept on going, getting funnier and funnier. Until finally... Well, let me tell you what happened.

She was laughing so hard that her spleen got all swollen. I'm telling you. Swollen, like a balloon... Now, the spleen... I'm sure you know, the spleen... That spongy thing up by the stomach, near the heart, full of corpuscles and cells, and other stuff like that. Serious business, the spleen. Not something you fool around with. But I don't have to tell you... Anyway, my damn fool funny friend won't stop when he's ahead. He just keeps on going. Full speed! Attack! Charge!... It was awful, what happened. Really, you can't imagine.

Her spleen swells up so much that it starts pushing against the... the... whatever, which is way out of place, and pressing against her windpipe. I mean pressing, pressing... Like you wouldn't... Pfff! And there she is, trying to catch her breath, but she can't, because it's pressing... (If I had a pencil I could draw you a picture.) Pressing harder and harder... And her diaphragm... Her sternum, her... Enough, you idiot! Stop, for God's sake!... But he won't. He just keeps going, and her whatever it was keeps pressing against her windpipe... She gasps, she gurgles... But the air can't get through. So "bam!" Just like that! And she keels over. Dead...

Like they say, a story you could die laughing over. All well and good, but still...

Anyway, my friend isn't too happy. Just then the boss's wife comes running down the stairs, and she points her finger at him.

"You killed her!" she screams. "You beat her to death!"

"Says who?" my friend snaps back. "I just told her a funny story."

"With a blunt instrument?"

"With no instrument at all!"

And he tries to explain that she laughed herself to death.

The boss's wife doesn't think that's very funny.

"I've got a funny feeling you're going to pay for your funny business," she tells him.

Sure enough, the police come and size up the situation. They give my friend a funny look and drag him off to the station. And they put him through hell, for hours and hours. Hell, like you wouldn't believe...

"All right, what did you do to her?"

"Nothing. I told her a funny story."

"Sure... Sure..."

But what else could he say? It was the truth, after all.

"A story? What story? Tell us... Tell us your funny story."

"No, I won't!"

And so they grill him. But when I say "grill"... With your wallops to the head... "Take that, you swine!..." And the pincers, and the prods... And his toes mashed to a pulp... And the thousand watts in the face... And... Enough to drive him crazy. Which it did, believe me. After eighteen hours he breaks.

"I can't take it any more!" he groans. "I'll tell it! I'll tell it!... Send in the judge. I'll tell him my story."

Well, the judge comes in, grumbling. He tells them to leave him alone with the prisoner. So they all leave except for a big burly cop. Just in case, because you never know.

And my friend tells his story.

The judge listens, begins to smile, then chuckles, then chortles, then slaps his thigh, then doubles up... Soon he can't catch his breath, and he gestures to my friend to stop. He can't take it, he's had enough. But it's too late. He's done for. And he keels over... Dead.

The cop kicked the bucket too, but not till the next day, in a hospital bed.

It took him that much longer to understand it.

Meanwhile my friend... No names, no names... Well, there he was, brooding in his cell, eating himself up alive, if you know what I mean.

"I'm a menace, a bloody menace," he kept repeating. "That's all there is to it. Funny stories are my business, but that one's a bloody killer. If I tell it there won't be an audience left alive. And if I fix it, it won't still be the funniest story ever, the bloody masterpiece of funny stories! Damn! There's no hope. I'm done for."

Next morning, when they opened the door to his cell, they found him. He was dead.

He'd killed himself, poor thing.

All night long he'd kept telling himself his funny story.

So you see, since then... When you ask me to tell you a... Well, believe me... (*Shaking his head, and going off.*) Believe me...

Alexandre Breffort, *Une Histoire drôle*

Clean Out of Her Mind

She had always had an obsession with cleanliness, with the principles of hygiene observed to the letter. It was, so to speak, in her blood: a pure, unsullied, thoroughly French blood, I might add.

She had married rather late, at the age of thirty-two. No man had ever seemed to her fastidious enough to kiss her, touch her, or take her in his arms, let alone to share her bed.

In time, however, she had relented, though only after subjecting some twenty-odd suitors to interminable tests, fatiguing analyses, and bizarre sanitations.

And even then, before she would have sex with her husband—which she allowed to take place only once per season—she would have him completely disinfected from head to toe.

Nothing very surprising about that, since she regularly used to vacuum her lawn and polish the leaves of the two trees in her garden once a month. Not very surprising either that, one evening, she stabbed her husband to death when he had had the temerity to give her a hug without first washing his hands.

Her act was unpardonable, reprehensible in fact, since the gentleman she had married after such long indecision was a creature of the utmost delicacy of taste and temper, all pink and white and smooth all over, soft-spoken and mild-mannered, and himself, of course, no less of a hygiene fanatic than was she.

Next day, when the housekeeper arrived, our murderess didn't even see her come into the bedroom, engrossed as she was in scrubbing her husband's cadaver with steel wool and detergent.

They arrested her at once, but when she saw that they were going to lock her up in a cell of debatable cleanliness, and what's more, without a washroom, she hurled herself at her guards and almost tore them and bit them to shreds, tooth and nail.

Thanks to that violent and hysterical outburst she was hauled off to a psychiatric clinic and put in a straitjacket.

And when she came to and felt it, wrapped around her, coarse and grimy against her skin, she lost her mind for good. Or at least what little of her mind she still had left.

Jacques Sternberg, *Hygiène*

Love in Bloom

He loved nothing as much as his flowers and his plants, except for the woman he'd been living with for several years.

His whole world amounted to only those two passions. Equally intense and admitting of no other. Often, indeed, he would spend long, long moments at a time gazing first at his tropical flowers and then at the body of his exquisite mistress, at his rare plants and her no-less-bewitching face, and he would feel quite overwhelmed by both: his flower-woman and his oh-so-feminine flora.

Then, one day, rumors began to spread throughout the countryside, from house to house, and finally to the nearby village. It was noted with considerable surprise that no one had seen the plant lover's lady in rather a long time, though in the past the neighbors and merchants would see her now and then, even if she kept her distance and seldom, if ever, spoke.

An investigation took place.

Plied with insistent questions from the start, he grew more and more suspect the more evasively he answered them—that is, when he deigned to say anything at all.

They combed his house from top to bottom but unearthed nothing in the least suspicious. They moved his furniture about, dug up his cellar, poked holes here and there in walls, but no trace of a body or blood was to be found. They turned over the earth in his garden, pulled up the tiles in his courtyard and the floorboards in his shed, but didn't discover a thing. Not a clue. They even tried hoeing up the artificial soil in his huge tropical hothouse, but the teeming, chaotic growth of trees and vines, plants and flowers, intertwining over every square inch of that lush, impenetrable jungle, made any digging whatever quite out of the question.

Finally they called the whole matter off, even offered their apologies.

And yet, had the police dared venture deep into the dank and stifling world of that enormous hothouse... Ah, but they would have seen what the plant lover had been seeing for weeks, what he had been gazing at for hours on end, ecstatic, caught between his morbid bliss and the delights of his mad passion.

They would have seen, there, beneath the parasol shade of a gigantic leaf, a tapered, delicately chiseled hand that seemed stuck in among the petals of a diaphanous flower; and farther, an ivory arm, so slender as to serve as a stake for a fragile plant, snaking up from the soil toward heights beyond its reach; and lower down, several fingers, almost translucent, grafted onto the stems of poisonous orchids; and there, still farther off, the two pallid hemispheres of a marble-perfect rump, like a basin turned upside down, and from between them, rising long, the stalk of a tropical flower.

And especially, there, in the middle of a murky little pool, the astonishing sight of a woman's upright head, haughty and ghastly pale, that seemed imprisoned in its beauty, embedded in the curves and folds of a giant water lily.

Jacques Sternberg, *L'Horticulteur*

II

Of Ills, Potions, Cures, Quacks, *&* Saviors

The Heroic Deed of Doctor Hallidonhill
or
Conspicuous Consumption

The extraordinary case of Dr. Hallidonhill is about to be tried before the criminal court of London. Here are the facts.

On May 20th last, the two vast waiting-rooms of the renowned specialist—caretaker, so to speak, of every manner of pulmonary disorder—were, as usual, filled to overflowing with prospective patients, each with his numbered admission ticket in hand.

Standing at the entrance, in a long black frock coat, the doctor's money-tester would take the required two guineas from each, pound the coins with a single hammer blow on an elegant anvil, and, finding them genuine, would automatically bellow out a Britannic "All right!"

In his glass-enclosed study, lined round with imposing tropical plants in huge Japanese pots, a brittle little Dr. Hallidonhill had just sat down behind his desk. At a small table by his side, his factotum was noting down in shorthand the master's terse prescriptions.

In the doorway—padded in a red velvet tacked with gold nail-heads—stood the doctor's valet, a bull-necked giant whose function it was to escort the tottering consumptives out the door, one after another, and into a special chair-fitted lift that would lower them to the exit. (All this, of course, after the ceremonial "Next!" had been duly intoned.)

The patients would come in, blank-stared and bleary-eyed, stripped to the waist, clothes over their arm. In no time the stethoscope would be applied, front and back.

"Huff! Puff!... Breathe in!..." the doctor began. "Good

God! Never mind!... Hopeless case!..." And he grumbled: "I'm a doctor, not a coroner! I'm not here to sign death certificates!..." Then, turning to the patient: "My good man, your left superior pulmonary lobe will disarticulate within a week, and you can expect to expectorate it forthwith! As for the right lung, it has more holes than a sieve!... Terribly sorry!... Next!..."

The valet was about to "dispose of the patient," as they usually put it, when the eminent practitioner, thwacking his forehead as if suddenly inspired, added abruptly, with an enigmatic smile:

"One minute... Are you rich?"

"Mul-ti-mil-lion-aire!" rattled the tearful unfortunate, whom Hallidonhill had just dispatched so summarily from the planet.

"Aha!... In that case... Have them bundle you off to Victoria Station... Take the eleven o'clock express to Dover... The ferry to Calais... The train to Marseilles... With a sleeping-car... Heated... Then to Nice! And in Nice, for six months you eat watercress, day and night! No bread, no wine, no fruit, no meat!... Nothing but watercress! With a teaspoon of rainwater every other day... Iodized, of course!... And watercress, watercress, watercress! Understand? Minced, mashed, stewed, puréed... It's your only chance... And a wild one at that, because frankly... I think all the claims are pure rubbish. But for you... Since you're half dead already... Well, it can't hurt... Next! Next!..."

The consumptive Croesus was tucked gently away in the padded lift, and the usual procession of scrofulous pleuritics, laryngitics, and bronchitics began once again.

Now, six months passed, and on the fifth of November, at the stroke of nine, there burst into the sanctum of the Prince of Science a strapping, rotund, well-fed, well-furred colossus, no ticket in hand, parting the ranks of the pathetic clientele like a human torpedo, and whose lusty, jubilant voice shook the glass study walls and set the leaves of the tropical plants aquiver. The doctor, impassive in his black morning-coat, had, as usual, just sat down behind his desk. The giant, flinging his arms about his waist, lifted him up in the air like a feather, first silently bathing his pallid, beardless face with heartfelt tears, then smothering him with resounding kisses, again and again, first one cheek then the other, finally setting him down, swooning and half-strangled, back in his green chair.

"Two million? Is two million enough? Three million?" the giant roared, awesome flesh-and-blood testimonial. "I owe you my life. You've given me back my breath, my sunlight, my days, my nights, my appetite, my *joie de vivre!*... Everything! Everything!... Tell me how much you want, and it's yours! No fee is too high! Please! How can I ever thank you?"

"Good God!" gasped the doctor, feebly, after a moment of stunned panic. "Who is this madman? Get him out of here! Get him out!"

"No, no!" growled the giant, with a pugilist's glower that froze the valet in his tracks. "You don't recognize me, doctor, do you? You... My savior!... It's me! The skeleton! The hopeless case!... Watercress, watercress, watercress! Remember? Six months in Nice!... Well, I'm back!... See? Look at your handiwork!... Here... Listen..."

And he thumped his thorax with a pair of fists that could smash the skulls of prime Middlesex bulls.

"Wh... Wh... What?" stammered the doctor, leaping to his feet. "You... You mean, you... That... That cadaver?"

"Yes, yes!" whooped the giant. "A thousand times yes! It's me! Me! Me!... Why, the minute I got off the boat last night, I ordered your statue... In bronze!... And that's not all!... I'm going to see to it that you're buried at Westminster Abbey!"

He let himself sink into a vast expanse of sofa. The springs squealed and groaned.

"Ah," he sighed, with a blissful smile of utter beatitude. "Life is good... Life is good..."

Two quick words from the doctor, under his breath, and both valet and factotum disappeared out the door. Once alone with his late cadaver, newly risen from the dead, a pale Dr. Hallidonhill, coldly calm and collected, leered at the giant for a few silent moments. Then he muttered, bizarrely:

"I say... Let me brush that fly from your temple..."

And, lunging toward him, he pulled a small revolver from his pocket and discharged two bullets, point blank, into his left temporal artery.

The giant fell in a heap, skull shattered, strewing the carpet with his ever-so-grateful cerebellum, and thrashing the floor for a minute or so in a flurry of flailing palms.

Scissors hacked with blind abandon—through fur piece, coat, waistcoat, shirt—and laid bare the giant's chest, which the doctor, intent, proceeded to slice from neck to navel with one slash of his scalpel.

A quarter-hour later, when the constable entered his study and asked Dr. Hallidonhill to be so good as to come along with him, he found him calmly sitting behind his desk, powerful magnifying glass in hand, examining a pair of gigantic twin lungs lying in a puddle of blood, trying to discover the ultra-miraculous palliative and restorative properties of watercress.

"You see, constable," said the Prodigy of Science, rising to his feet, "I deemed it essential to offer up this victim. Only an autopsy, performed posthaste, could reveal to me a secret potentially beneficial to our degenerate air-breathing branch of the zoological tree. And that, sir, is why I did not hesitate—I confess—TO SACRIFICE, AS

YOU CAN SEE, MY CONSCIENCE… TO MY DUTY."

No need to add that the eminent doctor has been released on bail—a purely nominal sum—since his freedom can benefit us far more than his incarceration. And now his curious case is to be judged by the British courts. Ah! What eloquent wonders of legal defense all Europe is about to read!

We have every reason to hope that this sublime assassination will not lead its hero to the Newgate gallows. For the English, like ourselves, are enlightened enough to realize that, in this day and age, an all-embracing love of tomorrow's Humanity—even at the price of today's Individual—is all that is needed to vindicate the noble and selfless extremists of Science.

Auguste de Villiers de l'Isle-Adam,
L'Héroïsme du Docteur Hallidonhill

Great Expectorations
or
T.B. or Not T.B.

Not exactly the cheeriest of chaps, this eminent Professor Koeniger...

As a result of the somber scientist's most recent experiments, it has come to light—a trifle dimly, perhaps—that no one will have the good fortune to avoid tuberculosis unless he undertakes to spend the rest of his days enclosed in a glass bubble, blown fresh from the fire, and in which one has taken the wise precaution of creating a perfect vacuum.

A rather vexatious condition, to be sure... Especially for those obliged by their occupations to absent themselves from their places of residence... One thinks, for example, of steeplechase jockeys, among others.

Each time said Professor Koeniger passes by one of those signs proclaiming "Spitting Forbidden," he shrugs his shoulders and mutters through clenched teeth that the sanitary measure thus imposed is indeed the most useless and absurd that he has ever encountered in his already lengthy career in the field of public hygiene.

The spitter, he asserts, is hazardous only after the fact, since, in order to be a source of danger, his spittle must have time to dry and combine with the atmosphere.

But the cougher!... The sneezer!... Ah! These jolly fellows are another matter altogether!

The likes of them deliver right to your doorstep—in a manner of speaking—and utterly without stint, a veritable downpour of droplets, every one a diminutive aquarium harboring myriads of bacilli, each one ready for action!

The good professor has spared neither his time nor his pains to specify certain aspects of the problem.

You may judge for yourselves...

I quote:

"In a room whose air is standing undisturbed, the bacilli propelled by the cougher or the sneezer remain in suspension for almost one hour. If, on the other hand, the air is stirring, it takes them a full hour and a half to reach the ground... A person who coughs or sneezes is capable of projecting a spray of microbes over a distance of five or six meters. And most distressing is the fact that this death-dealing shower 'fans out,' as it were, spreading to the left, to the right, and even behind its perpetrator."

And that, my dear friends, is far from being the whole story!

Speech!... Yes, speech itself... That gift of the Creator... Speech!... That faculty that sets us above the wild beasts... Even speech is rich in pestilential potential!

Let us listen once again to our savant's own words.

I quote:

"The number of microbes projected by the speech act is a function of the subject's manner of speaking, the force of his utterance, the clarity of his enunciation, and his accent."

Yes, my friends, even his accent!

The professor, it seems, has ascertained that those who speak with a harsh, clipped accent possess a projectile capacity of disquieting abundance.

In this regard the English, the Germans, the Scandinavians,

and especially the Flemish, are to be assiduously avoided... Like the plague, I am tempted to add.

Vowels, we are assured, are less bacterial than consonants.

Among the latter, it is the labials, dentals, and linguals that furnish the most copious spray... Especially, the professor informs us, the letters t, p, k, b, z, and f.

That being the case, a word of caution is in order to all those of you hygienically concerned.

Be sure, in your conversations, to use only those words from which the aforementioned deadly consonants have been rigorously excluded.

Never, for example, tell your interlocutor (or -trix), even if the situation categorically demands it, that you saw a "pretty, fat, cocky baby zebra," all nine syllables of which are lethal.

Clearly we had all best be circumspect in what we say and how we say it.

Now, who, I ask you, stands to gain from this terrifying new scourge?

Why, the deaf mutes, by Jove!... Yes, our dear deaf-mute friends, who, even as I speak, are already being fought over by timorous families for their prophylactic presence...

Personally I am delighted, as you might well imagine, to see all these fine folk profit from such a windfall!

Alphonse Allais, *La Revanche des sourds-muets*

The Germ of the Problem

I had just politely ordered my two boiled eggs in the unpretentious café where I breakfast every morning in most modest fashion, when, all of a sudden, a tall young man at the table next to mine—blond, gentle-looking, a trifle timid—stood up and, without a word, pointed a revolver at my heart and fired.

Fortunately, owing either to the inferior manufacture of the weapon or to the shoddy nature of the ammunition with which it was loaded, the bullet, rather than lodge in my anatomy, merely grazed one of my ribs—especially solid in my case—causing no more than a nasty flesh wound.

However, since I was, indeed, bleeding, I decided not to dally in fruitless recriminations, but rather—surveying the damage—to repair (so to speak) to the nearest apothecary's.

With an attentiveness that I hasten to acknowledge here and now in public, our good purveyor of pills and potions wasted no time in stopping the bleeding, though not before he had quipped, unfortunate punster that he was: "It's like Aquinas said: 'No effect without a proper gauze,'" repeating as he bandaged: "Proper gauze... proper gauze..."

In the meantime, my assassin, the tall young man—blond, gentle-looking, a trifle timid—had followed me to the apothecary's and was standing by as the latter bound my wound, even offering to help in whatever way he could.

When the bandaging was done, the assassin and I returned to our common café, attacking our breakfasts with an uncommon appetite, famished, as you can imagine, by the whole nasty affair.

"Would you be good enough to tell me, *cher monsieur*," I asked him, "just what it was that prompted such untoward behavior?"

"With pleasure, *cher monsieur!* Especially since, like our silly apothecary friend, I too had 'proper gauze.' No less than that Swedish student last week. From the Society for the Prevention of Cruelty to Animals... Remember? The one who shot the toreador in the bull-ring."

"Oh?" I replied, "I'm afraid I don't quite see..."

"When I heard you ordering two boiled eggs it was more than my animal lover's heart could bear... I'm sure you understand."

"Well, not really," I protested. "I grant you, eggs are a form of living matter. But I hardly think they feel any pain. Or, indeed, anything else."

"Quite so. And it's not the eggs that concern me. What I pity are the millions of microscopic creatures—even ultra-microscopic—happily frolicking about in the water, carefree and innocent, only to be subjected, without the slightest warning, to temperatures that they were never brought up to expect, and that quite overpower their fragile constitutions. After all," he concluded, "you can't have boiled eggs with boiling the water."

"Yes," I nodded. "Perhaps..."

"Not 'perhaps!' There's no question. It's all very kind and generous to pity a poor bull. But a bull, *cher monsieur*, is just that: one bull. Whereas, when you brew yourself a single cup of camomile, you're wreaking more havoc—more suffering, more torture—than in all of the bullrings in the world, for centuries."

"That's a horrible thought," I agreed. "Tell me, what's your solution?"

"Very simple," he replied. "When the demands of life are

such that you absolutely must boil water, be good enough to add a strong dose of cocaine. That way, at least, the poor creatures won't have to suffer."

★

I've seen fit to take the young man's advice.

Which is why those who honor my table at dinner find that the food has an extraordinary taste, and experience a curious discomfort as they leave.

Alphonse Allais,
Il ne faut faire aux microbes nulle peine, même légère

Patient Cure Thyself
or
The Unkindest Cut of All

"Harumph!… You can get dressed now," said the eminent Dr. Patentson, with a nod of the head, as his patient, scrawny and wheezing, looked him anxiously in the eye.

"And what should I do?" asked the latter.

"Whatever you like. It won't make any difference. You're done for."

"Damn! That's nasty news!" murmured the patient, visibly distressed.

"Yes, well… That's just the way it is." And the eminent Dr. Patentson, picking up from his desk the register in which he kept note of his clientele, took a red pencil and summarily crossed out the poor soul's name as the latter, not without considerable effort, replaced his shirt on his fleshless torso and took his leave.

And, casting a proud and satisfied glance at his latest invention—a microbe dissection kit that lacked only a few finishing touches—the eminent Dr. Patentson donned his long white coat and left his office in the New York hospital where he served as chief of medicine, ready to go make his rounds of the wards.

Six months later, a gentleman came crossing the threshold of the eminent physician's office, much to the latter's rather bemused surprise, since the visitor seemed, to all appearances, perfectly healthy.

"Are you ill?"

"Not in the slightest! I'm completely cured. In fact, that's what I've come to tell you. Six months ago you told me I was done for…"

"And you didn't die? Come now!" intoned the eminent physician.

Indeed, it was the first time that a patient had so brazenly flouted his diagnosis. After a moment or two of reflection he continued:

"You say you're completely cured?"

"Completely."

"I'm sorry, that simply cannot be! Please be good enough to undress!"

The erstwhile invalid let the eminent physician listen to his chest, all the while explaining the treatment he had undergone: a very simple one, in fact, recommended to him by an old crone of his acquaintance.

Patentson could not believe his eyes or ears. "It's not possible," he assured him. "It flies in the face of every rule of the profession…" And, with a gesture: "Please be so kind as to step into my laboratory."

The laboratory in question, replete with instruments for piercing, slicing, and sawing, looked quite like a torture chamber, with a marble table in the center of which the eminent physician invited the gentleman to lie down, grumbling as he did so: "It's not right to muck about with Science like that, my friend."

Then, palpating his subject's anatomy here and there, the eminent physician picked up a scalpel and stood scratching his nose with it, like one deep in thought. The patient, meanwhile, was smiling smugly at the eminent physician's annoyance, promising himself to relate the account the length and breadth of New York society. But suddenly Patentson, with extraordinary precision, plunged the scalpel with which he had been toying for a moment into the gentleman's heart. The latter, without so much as a peep, grew quite motionless all at once, his smile still frozen on his lips.

At which point Patentson, putting on his apron, artfully dissected the cadaver and stood for a long time contemplating its scarred lungs. At length, quite amazed, he mumbled:

"Damn! That's a good one! He was right. He was cured. Completely..."

Léon Xanrof, *Incrédulité* [1]

---

[1]The reader will be struck by the obvious similarity, details aside, between this piece and the preceding work of Villiers de l'Isle Adam (pp. 63 – 67), which apparently also inspired still another, later version by Guillaume Apollinaire (pp. 94 – 97).

Double Crossed

It's curious how tastes change over the years. For centuries they've been pitying Christ for having his cross to bear. Well, today it's all the rage... Not to bear one on your shoulders, but to wear one on your lapel... The cross of the Order of This... The cross of the Order of That... Whatever... I know dozens of good staunch liberals, believe me—independent as can be—who would give their eyeteeth to take an order from somebody. No matter what order, as long as there's a cross...

Le Bouzeur and his chum Ciliace were precisely two such aspirants, each with only a single thought in mind: to enter the orders, so to speak—any of the orders of the bemedaled lapel—feeling, as they did, that some honorific distinction was needed to enhance the qualities with which Nature had endowed them. But, being a little young for the Legion of Honor, they were setting rather more modest sights on one of those foreign decorations... The kind our civil servants pick up, without too much trouble, for missions here and there...

One day, while they were off in the countryside—resting up from the rigors to which final exams were, doubtless, subjecting their colleagues—they were discussing that very subject as they ambled along the Seine:

"What do you suppose you have to do to get decorated?" Le Bouzeur was musing.

"Know someone high up," replied Ciliace.

"If you've saved someone's life, do they give you a medal?"

"Sure... Like I say, if you know the right people... Why?

Have you ever…?"

"Yes… Once, in a fire…"

"No! Really?"

"Yes… Myself… But I guess… No," Le Bouzeur sighed. "No… I guess that doesn't count."

"Not hardly!" Ciliace agreed.

But just at that moment, an idea hit him:

"Wait… Can you swim?"

"Of course!" Le Bouzeur answered. "What do you take me for?"

"Well then… You could jump into the river and start to drown…"

"I could?"

"And I could save you… And they'd give me a medal!"

"Oh? And what about me? You jump in, why don't you?"

"Me?" Ciliace objected. "Then how would I get my medal?"

"Damn!" Le Bouzeur muttered. "You'd think there must be an idiot somewhere who'd drown so both of us could save him… It's a small enough favor…"

Then, pointing upstream:

"Like that fisherman over there… Standing up in his boat… Wouldn't you think he could slip?"

"What a brilliant idea!" Ciliace chimed in. "If we just gave that rope a little tug… The one his boat's attached to…"

"Exactly! He'd flop into the drink..."

"And we'd save him..."

"And both get medals!" Le Bouzeur concluded, slapping Ciliace on the back in such a flurry of enthusiasm that his friend was nearly sent "flopping" prematurely into said "drink" himself.

The project was difficult, and not without its risks—to say nothing of rather questionable ethical considerations. But, blinded as they were by the passions of the moment, the two friends paid no mind, and with infinite precaution edged their way toward their victim.

The individual in question was the utter personification of the meek, inoffensive Parisian fisherman—all baiting and waiting, and waiting unabating... The type about whom it is said—and wrongly, I might add—that his line has a fool at one end and a sucker at the other. I say "wrongly," because there's hardly a fish in the Seine enough of a sucker to bite at his bait.

Well, be that as it may... There the fisherman stood, at the prow of his bobbing boat—tied to a stake in the river (his boat, that is) and, at the same time, moored to shore—deep in contemplation of the little red float.

"Beware!" seem to whisper the waves, lapping in the sun.

"Beware!" whistles the wind, caressing his spindly legs and his woebegone straw hat.

"Beware!" creak the little pebbles, strewn along the shore, beneath the tread of the two students' feet...

But, still lost in contemplation, the fisherman doesn't hear...

Then a cry... And another... And cries echoing in the distance...

A splash in the water... The fisherman disappears...

There, standing on the bank, two selfless heroes, without a second thought, strip off their jackets, about to dive in...

But wait!... What's that?... O miracle of miracles! There, just below the surface... A yellowish mass... Rising up from the water, it becomes a straw hat... And beneath it, a head... A face, terrified, livid... Then, finally, a torso, as the fisherman—standing waist-deep in the water, staggers toward the shore...

"Oh no!" objects Le Bouzeur. "No, damn it!"

"Not on your bloody life!" an outraged Ciliace concurs.

And the pair plunge in... Well, "run in," really, since the water is barely up to their knees... And they grab the poor fisherman, befuddled and bewildered, each by an arm, and drag him bodily toward the middle of the river.

"Help!" screams the poor soul, frantic, still pale with fright. "He—"

As he opens his mouth again, a violent submersion renders him suddenly speechless.

But he struggles... Pokes his head up... This time his face is scarlet.

"Hel—"

Again he's submerged by our two courageous friends. By now a crowd of spectators, running from every direction, line the banks of the river and peer, with bated breath, to witness the daring rescue.

A third time the fisherman's head comes to the surface. He's green... He tries to scream, to shout... In vain. And again he disappears with a splash beneath the waves...

Ah, but not for long. Our two intrepid heroes take unprecedented pains to dredge him up from the depths and haul him in to shore, where they lay him out on the ground, prostrate and inert.

The fisherman lies there, quite as silent as his fish, and every color of the rainbow.

A chatter of speculation goes running through the crowd... Accident?... Suicide?...

Le Bouzeur and Ciliace begin to wonder if they may have gone a trifle too far, and take care not to let any of the bystanders approach to try to revive their catch.

From mouth to mouth, one murmur of admiration:

"Fine young men!... Brave young heroes!..."

"Damnation!" think the pair. "If he's dead, there go our medals!"

And they rub, and whack, and thwack, and massage...

At last their victim opens one eye... Then the other... Then his mouth... But one glimpse of his two benefactors, and all at once a look of sheer horror glazes over his face. He tries to push them away...

"Goddamn!" thinks Le Bouzeur. "If this idiot spills the beans..."

Just then Ciliace shouted (it was obviously his day for brilliant ideas!):

"He'd better have a good hot drink! Something to warm him up..."

So saying, he took the poor man under one arm, and, with Le Bouzeur on the other, the two of them whisked him across the way to a neighboring wine shop.

But not without an effort.

The fisherman, gradually coming to his senses, grew more and more reluctant, and even seemed intent on escaping from his rescuers, who, showering him with attention, kept tugging at his arms.

"Leave me... Leave me alone..." whimpered the poor devil, whose return to the living had sparked a glimmer of revolt.

"It's for your own good, monsieur," they assured him. And the crowd, encouraging, urged him on.

They finally dragged him into the wine shop and ordered him a toddy. But while the wine was heating, the owner, who knew him, began to ask him questions:

"What in the name of... How did it happen?"

"Please!" Ciliace jumped in. "After all he's been through... Not now!... Later!... Can't you see he's tired?"

"No, no... I'm not... I'm not..." the fisherman moaned. And, pointing a feeble finger at Ciliace and Le Bouzeur: "It's those two... Those two... They're the ones—"

"Yes," Ciliace interrupted. "We're the ones who saved him! Thank heaven we were in time!" Then, turning to the fisherman, he whispered in his ear: "Keep your mouth shut and I'll give you a hundred francs, understand?"

On the other side, Le Bouzeur had grabbed him by the collar, muttering under his breath:

"Say another word and I'll strangle you, do you hear?"

And he added, out loud:

"Better get him out of those wet clothes right away!"

Now, whether tempted by the promise of the one hundred francs—problematic, at best, coming from Ciliace—or whether convinced by the force of Le Bouzeur's persuasion, whatever the reason, the fisherman held his tongue. As if in a trance, he gazed at the two friends while his clothes were peeled off to dry, replaced by a flannel undershirt and one of the owner's wife's voluminous old petticoats. All of which rather gave him the look of a trained chimpanzee...

And as he was fed his toddy—and a second, and a third, and a fourth—his blank stare never wavered.

Impatient, Le Bouzeur crawled under the chair to see if the poor thing hadn't possibly sprung a leak.

But finally, in time, his eyes began to close, and his head began to nod.

And, as he sat dreaming, no doubt, of a hundred francs, the two friends took their leave—though (needless to say) not the check for the toddies.

The fisherman could never quite remember, when he woke, just how the whole thing happened. But what's clear is that he feels no great gratitude toward his rescuers.

As for Ciliace and Le Bouzeur, it should be mentioned that a private society for the recognition of acts of valor has recently awarded them each a handsome certificate.

But neither one, as yet, has dared pin it to his lapel.

Léon Xanrof, *Un Sauvetage*

Medic-à-la-Mode

or

A Modern Surgeon's New Cures for Old Ills

Modern surgery has made enormous progress. It would be a mark of senility to deny it.

The lancet and the scalpel, wielded by skillful hands, penetrate, probe, and perform their operations in every cranny of our being. Surgeons today excel in locating the ill, isolating it, and subjecting it to the most scientific of techniques. Should you, for instance, have a blister on your back, it is perfectly commonplace for them to slice open your belly in order to gain access to it and attack it from the other side.

As for anesthetics, they are used today so easily and expertly that it is almost a sport to have oneself put to sleep. Thanks to cocaine, for example, people have quite lost the habit of enduring pain, and the least little physical inconvenience has become a source of suffering. As a result, they turn to chloroform when about to have a pedicure, and routinely go to hospital when obliged to take a footbath.

Among the surgical luminaries of our day, the celebrated Dr. Ileon is certainly one of the most luminous. A statistical analysis of his operations over the last thirty-five years should prove of interest. Of every hundred patients, a mere 2.8—or two and eight tenths—failed to survive. Of those remaining, 6.7 definitively recovered, whereas 90.5 eventually succumbed to a variety of complications, notwithstanding the notable success of his surgical procedures.

Dr. Ileon is also much concerned with public sanitation and hygiene. In this regard his accomplishments are legion. It is to him, for example, that we owe the invention—no less distinguished than that of our streetcorner urinals—of sidewalk spitting stations.

Furthermore, he has proposed to the government that it do away with coins made of metal, known to spread numerous cutaneous infections, and that it replace them with little disks fashioned out of coal and previously treated with phenyl salicilate.

He is also responsible for another hygienic innovation soon to make its appearance in our restaurants and cafés: namely, the disinfectant fly-repellent serving-tray calculated to protect the eating public from the many diseases spread hither and yon by said insect's minuscule feet.

Now, it happens that Dr. Ileon, when vacationing in a certain port town, as is his wont, pays frequent visits to the local seamen's infirmary in order to scrutinize attentively the nurses' and orderlies' hygienic precautions. Not long ago, as he was making his daily rounds one morning, a gray-bearded individual—face battered and bruised—was carried in on a stretcher, having been found along the waterfront lying motionless by the shore.

It was generally assumed that the seaman was, in local parlance, three sheets to the wind. Dr. Ileon, however, was unwilling to accept a diagnosis as facile as mere inebriation. A close examination of the subject's grimy and bloated face revealed to him, indeed, a rather characteristic swelling of the right cheek.

Wasting no time, he asked to have his surgical instruments brought to him, much to the anticipated delight of interns and staff, awed at the prospect of seeing the renowned practitioner ply his craft.

The doctor proceeded to make a cross-shaped incision, plunged his thumb and forefinger deep inside, and, after scarcely a moment, withdrew a sizable wad of chewing-tobacco that had been lodged between the patient's cheek and gum.

The operation has been the subject of spirited discussion at the infirmary, and in Paris as well, throughout the entire medical community. Dr. Ileon, in an effort to have the final word, is about to publish a paper entitled: "The surgical procedure for the extraction of tobacco from a sailor's mouth without necessitating the opening of the patient's lips and jaws."

Tristan Bernard, *Hygiène et chirurgie*

Woes Be Gone

or

A Druggist's Young Wife Writes Home

Chère maman,

If I haven't written to you recently it's only because we were having some hard times and I didn't want to worry you. At the beginning of the month we didn't even have a sou to our name, and you'll never know how close you came to reading our obituaries in the local paper.

My poor Henri never got the three hundred francs he was promised. We owed all the shopkeepers money and none of them would give us any more credit. So last Thursday we were all set to take strychnine, the two of us. In fact, Henri had already gone downstairs to the laboratory to mix it up.

But first I got down on my knees, maman, and I started to pray as hard as I could. Well, would you believe it? It was like a miracle. The doorbell rang and a man came running into the pharmacy. God must have heard me. He told me—the man, that is—that they had just discovered a case of diphtheria in town.

The next day they found another one. This time it was the mayor himself. Well, you know how rich he is. You can imagine all the things he had us send: iodine, applicators, pills, everything. Anyway, it was enough to pay the butcher.

But that wasn't all. Our good luck just kept on coming. One of the help from the château fell off a horse and broke his leg. They had to amputate. That was good for ten packages of antiseptic dressing, mercuric chloride, sticking plaster... Three whole yards of sticking plaster, maman! Then that very same night one of our neighbors

got bitten by a mad dog! A rabid one, I'm happy to tell you... Just in time to pay for all of little Gaston's schoolbooks and things.

Last night we even went to see a play. Henri said we could afford it thanks to the terrible outbreak of diarrhea that afternoon at the old people's home.

Well, enough for now. Hugs and kisses, maman. Kiss papa for me.

Your loving daughter

PS   Oh! After all that good news something awful was bound to happen. I found out that the priest, Père Galouche, has died. He was such a fine man, and always in horrible pain with his liver. You could count on the attacks like clockwork. He used to spend a fortune on morphine with us.

Tristan Bernard, *Lettre d'une jeune pharmacienne*

Weight for the Doctor
or
Reductio ad Absurdum

People will never get tired making fun of the medical profession. Still, I think it's safe to say that doctors have never been as knowledgeable and devoted as they are today.

It's just that we don't do what they tell us.

You go see them as if they're saviors, and then, if you're not cured in a week you stop following their instructions. Then you say: "Bah! That Dr. So-and-So didn't do anything for me..."

The fact is you didn't listen. If you'd followed his instructions to the letter he would have cured you.

Say you wanted to lose weight and he told you to go on a diet, for example... Even fast, maybe... Well, you should have listened... You should have fasted for months. Four... Eight... As long as it took...

Anyway, let me get to the point... You know my friend Siméon? The big one with the beard and the long overcoat... Of course you know him... Well, four years ago he came to see me. He knew I was friends with all the bigwig Paris doctors...

Now, back then Siméon weighed almost three hundred pounds, and he decided he should reduce. So I gave him the name and address of my old friend, Dr. Belartur... You know the one... Rue Lafayette... Well, he goes to see him... Belartur examines him, head to toe, and prescribes a treatment he says never fails. A good, vigorous two-hour walk every morning and evening... Fine... Six weeks later Siméon was twenty-five pounds lighter.

The only problem was that his ankles have always been too weak for that big body of his. He couldn't walk anymore... Couldn't take another step... His feet were all swollen... Like balloons... So he comes to see me, and I give him the name of my friend, Dr. Schuetzmer... You know the one... The German foot doctor who has you stick your feet in wet mud or something... Well, not mud exactly... Some mixture of wet clay or other... Anyway, Siméon takes the treatment for three months, and by the time it's over his feet are cured. Completely... A hundred percent perfect!

"Ah!" he tells me one day. "I only wish I could do something about this sore throat I can't get rid of!"

Because, the truth of the matter is that, by getting his feet so wet in all that mud... Or whatever... Well, he'd caught some kind of terrible infection of the larynx, and he was always in awful pain, poor thing.

"No problem," I tell him. "Nothing easier to cure..." And I mention my friend Dr. Cholamel... You know the one... Cholamel... The one who discovered that a lot of sore throats come from bad circulation in the vocal cords... And he uses some electrical machine or other to get the blood moving... Anyway, Siméon took his treatment, and in just a few months... Voilà!... Completely cured... No more sore throats!

The only problem is... You see, everyone in his family has some special kind of nerve problem... All of them... And electricity makes it worse, so... Well, he kept getting these terrible attacks... Like fits, you know what I mean... Three or four times a day...

"Look," I told him. "You can't just ignore it... Really... You've got to do something... Go see my friend Dr. Langlevent... Mention my name... He'll fix you up in no time."

So he did. And Langlevent gave him something or other with bromide in it... But you know about bromide, and how bad it is for the stomach... Practically destroys it... Digestion? Pfff!... Forget it… Well, anyone will tell you that with stomach trouble you should-n't waste a minute. Dr. Biridoff is your man… Professor Biridoff, that is… My friend… You know the one… A month or two with him and your stomach is back on its feet…

Well, I sent Siméon to go see the professor. He examined him and put him on a high starch diet. Hardly any meat… Almost no wine… Just water, and lots of mashed up things… Beans, potatoes, peas… Purée of this, purée of that… Sure enough it worked. It did-n't take more than a couple of months before his stomach was as good as new.

Talk about being happy! I ran into him one day on the stairs as he was coming up to thank me… Panting… Because he was so fat… Damn! What do you expect? From all that starch… And he tells me now he weighs three hundred twenty pounds! Give or take… Even more than before…

"Too much! Too much!" I tell him. "You'd better watch that and see if you can't—"

But before I can finish Siméon goes "Ha! If I try to lose weight again they're going to make me walk, and my ankles are going to swell, and… and so on and so forth…"

"Who said anything about walking?" I tell him. "There are plenty of other ways to lose weight… Believe me… Tomorrow you and I are going to see my friend Dr. Lerenchéry…"

So we did, next day. And Lerenchéry told him what he had to do was lots and lots of horseback riding. Not just any old nag, mind you… And not just a nice little ride around the park either… Oh no!… Lerenchéry wrote him out a whole prescription… A dozen pages… With the exact times to go, the exact number of trots, the exact number of gallops… How many, how long… Practically down to the second… Well, Siméon went to the stable and picked himself out a horse. A real stallion… Big, strong… Full of life… And he began his exercise…

That was three days ago, and already he's taken off eighty pounds. Talk about results!...

Oh, I shouldn't forget to mention that, first time out, he fell off the horse and they had to amputate his left leg. Siméon's, that is... All eighty pounds of it...

Anyway, you see? He listened to the doctors... It's like I was saying... As long as you listen to them and do what they tell you, you're going to be just fine...

Tristan Bernard, *Les Médecins spécialistes*

Orange Aid
or
Curious Cure, Curious Doctor

The large Parisian dailies scarcely made even a mention of the James Kimberlin affair; a scandal that caused a tremendous stir from Australia to England. At most they reported that Dr. Kimberlin was arrested, charged with murder, tried, found guilty, and put to death.

I happened to be in Melbourne at the time, and I knew the doctor slightly. Having had the opportunity to meet him on a few occasions, I was able to appreciate his rare quality of mind, thoroughly devoted as it was to matters scientific.

His reputation as a physician was unequaled in all of Australia, and for that reason he had built up quite a thriving practice.

He was a man of about forty, endowed with unusual physical strength. A bachelor, he had led a life utterly above reproach, and it was generally agreed that he was free of every moral flaw.

Moreover, he was said to possess a certain unusual trait, one that will portray him perhaps far better than anything else one might tell about him. To wit, that he had such a frightful aversion to death that, should he be called to the bedside of a patient whose condition he deemed to be hopeless, he would simply refuse to treat him and would ask that one of his colleagues be summoned in his place. But such cases, one was quick to observe, were not at all common. Scarcely two times, in fact, in his long medical career, was he known to have thus demurred, quitting the sickroom without attempting the treatment requested. Rumor had it, therefore, that Dr. James Kimberlin had, indeed, cured every patient whom he had ever attended, and that, once he would proffer his advice or prescribe a remedy, the ill were sure to recover.

Such being the case, when the newspapers reported his arrest on a charge of murder, so blameless had Dr. James Kimberlin's career appeared to be that one and all claimed it was no doubt a terrible mistake. The evidence, however, soon convinced said one and all of his guilt; and they could only stand awestruck before the singular nature of the crime he had committed.

The circumstances thereof deserve to be known in detail. There is more to them by far than a banal news item. They present, rather, the most bizarre tableau imaginable of the manner in which the customary uses of professional behavior are able, suddenly, to pervert an upright and honorable soul, devoted above all to prolonging the life of his fellow human beings.

There is, happily, no need to fear a similar incident here in France. Our scientists are too enlightened, and their passion for their calling—strong though it be—is always overshadowed by their feelings of humanity. Such an event, indeed, could only occur in a young country; one in which a physician, clever and well-versed in his craft, enjoys such great prestige that he can, in time, come to consider himself above the law and free to dispose, as he chooses, of those very lives which he wrests from death itself.

Here then are the facts:

One Lee Lewes by name, a sheepherder by profession, had come in from the outback with a sizable fortune in gold—happy result of one drought-free year after another—and consumed by a long illness whose cause no one had been able to determine.

No sooner had he set foot in Melbourne than our shepherd consulted a number of physicians, all of whom pronounced his condition quite beyond help and advised him to prepare his last will and testament.

Lee Lewes made straight for a bar, intending first to spend all his gold and, afterwards, to shoot himself. So forlorn was his appearance, however, that the barmaid—a red-headed Irish miss—took pity on him and he told her his tale of woe. She in turn advised him not to waste a moment but to go consult Dr. James Kimberlin, lauding the latter's talents with such enthusiasm that, suddenly heartened, Lee Lewes gave up his thought of suicide, left his whiskey where it stood, and went to seek an audience with the celebrated physician.

Arriving at his door, he rings, presents himself, and recounts his ills. The doctor examines him and informs him, coldly, that there is nothing he can prescribe.

Lee Lewes insists.

"Please, doctor, I'm begging you. Don't give me up," he pleads. "If you do, you're sentencing me to death, nothing less."

James Kimberlin looks at him, feels a great pity for this man who, he knows, is doomed.

"Why shatter his hopes?" he thinks to himself. "At least let him die believing he can be saved." And, turning to him, he says: "Well then, drink orangeade. Yes, orangeade… Drink as much as you like…"

His peace of mind restored, a satisfied Lee Lewes took his leave, and Dr. Kimberlin, certain that the poor soul had little time to live, proceeded to forget the disturbing consultation.

In the meantime the patient began drinking his orangeades. And he drank them night and day. For a year on end he drank them, so much so that, in time, he had once again grown hale and hearty.

At which point, ready to return to the rude climes where he tended his sheep, Lee Lewes feels obliged to go visit his savior and express to him his gratitude.

And so he does, arriving at Dr. Kimberlin's study and bringing with him a costly gift. The physician barely recognizes him, quite unwilling to believe that such a curative miracle could ever have taken place.

But finally, unable to doubt the success of the orangeades that he had prescribed, and filled with a boundless curiosity regarding the reasons for such a cure, he asks Lee Lewes to step into his examining-room, where, gripped by a kind of professional dementia, he seizes his revolver, puts a bullet in his patient's brain, performs an autopsy, and examines his body in hopes of finding the cause of a disease whose essentials had eluded all his colleagues, but which he, quite unintentionally, had cured.

Once returning to his senses, however, and struck by the frightful enormity of his crime, he fled the city and wandered for several days in the country, until the police, learning of his disappearance and finding the cadaver, apprehended this unusual criminal in the sun-baked scrubland typical of the Australian landscape just as he was preparing to take his own life.

To make a long story short, James Kimberlin tried in vain to persuade the judges that he had acted in a fit of temporary insanity. He was found guilty and was obliged to pay with his life for his singular crime, committed as it was in a frenzy of scientific and utterly blameless curiosity.

Guillaume Apollinaire, *L'Orangeade*[1]

[1]See note, p. 76

Belly-Hoo
or
Doctors Sew-and-Sew

I crossed the threshold of the clinic, trying in vain to choke back my sobs.

In the superintendent's office an intern was fondling a pretty young thing in a pert white cap. A nurse, I imagine. I poked my head in and went "peek-a-boo!"

A stairway took me up to the second floor. On the landing, a drunk—the director, I later learned—pointed me to the operating room.

I opened the door. Good God, what a sight!

There, spread defenseless on a table, lay my poor friend Tom, with three coldblooded surgeons hovering about him, and looking like a leg of lamb just waiting to be sliced.

He gave me a wry little smile and beckoned me over. One of the surgeons offered me a chair. I sat down next to Tom and held his hand while they opened his belly with a stolid, stoic calm.

I'd got there, it seems, just in time for the opening.

It didn't take long. In five minutes it was over, and the wound was sewn up, neat as you please.

The three practitioners stood about shaking hands and congratulating one another. Meanwhile, out in the hall, you could hear the dim echo of the director's drunken ditties.

Suddenly, one of the surgeons grew frightfully pale.

"My glasses!" he cried.

They looked high and low, but there were no two ways about it. It was clear that the glasses must be in my poor friend's belly. So they took out the stitches. They opened him up. And they found the glasses sitting in his duodenum. Tom winced each time the needle pierced his skin.

No sooner was he sewn up again than the second surgeon went for his handkerchief, to wipe his brow. Went, that is, but didn't arrive. The handkerchief had disappeared, left behind in Tom's belly.

Again they unsewed. Again they resewed, after finding it in his small intestine.

The last surgeon, finally, breaking a weighty silence, said: "My friends, I think I could do with a pinch of snuff."

At which point a gargantuan sneeze from the patient, followed by others in a veritable volley, left no doubt where the snuffbox of said surgeon was lodging.

And, as the savage trio once again took up their scalpels, there arose a querulous and somewhat sardonic voice.

"Gentlemen," murmured my poor friend Tom, "if you have to keep this up, don't you think you'd do better just to sew on some buttons?"

Gabriel de Lautrec, *Le Ventre de Tom Joë*

III

Of Torsos, Limbs, Skulls,
&
Assorted Body Parts

The English Tongue

Tall, toothless, jaundiced, wrinkled, and stiff, the Englishwoman followed her feet into the post office.

Turning, she squeaked like a rusty wheelbarrow: "Come, come, Clara!"

Small, frail, flat-chested, and redheaded, with a mouth full of teeth, Clara too followed her feet behind her mistress.

The Englishwoman asked the clerk for sixty postage stamps, to stick on sixty letters addressed to sixty different people.

With five boney fingers she picked up the sixty stamps and repeated: "Come, come, Clara!"

Clara moved beside her with the grace of a locomotive.

Heels together, at attention, arms hanging by her sides, she raised her head and stuck out her tongue.

One after another, the Englishwoman—tall, toothless, jaundiced, wrinkled, and stiff—passed each stamp over small, frail, flat-chested, red-headed Clara's outstretched tongue, and stuck them, one by one, with a sharp little tap, on the sixty letters addressed to the sixty different people.

Then she strode toward the door, with another "Come, come, Clara!"

And both of them followed their respective feet out, disappearing like two shadows.

★

Recently I saw poor Clara again. She was still small, frail, flat-chested, and redheaded.

But her lips were stuck together, and her mouth was sealed shut...

Maurice Mac-Nab, *Old England*

The Blemished Bride
or
The Seat of the Problem

Did I tell you?... I'm getting married!... (*He opens out a newspaper and points to something.*) Here... This is where I found her... In the personal column... (*Reading.*) "Young lady... Twenty-two years old, pretty, excellent character... Two hundred thousand francs... One minor blemish..."

That's what it says... A blemish...

I have to admit, when I saw that word "blemish," it put me off a little.

Even minor... I mean...

After all, there are so many.

A wart on the nose? A personality trait? Some family flaw?... Pimples?

Well, blemish or not...

I'm not one to let a little thing like a blemish stand in the way... Between me and a young lady... Twenty-two years old, pretty, excellent character... Two hundred thousand francs...

So I asked for her hand in marriage.

Now, as far as the famous blemish is concerned, I found out all about it. Her mother took me aside one day and whispered in my ear...

It's a secret, in case you're wondering. Even the poor child herself doesn't know she has it. How could she? She's never seen it!

If I told you, you'd understand... (*Hesitating.*) Oh, all right... Why not? It's nothing to be ashamed of...

You see, it's a scar.

From a burn, that's all.

Yes, Arabelle, my fiancée... Arabelle de Labelle... A beautiful name... It has a nice ring to it... (*Blowing a kiss.*) Arabelle... Arabelle...

Anyway, as I was saying...

It seems the day of her baptism, when she was still just a baby... Well, she fell into a frying-pan... Bottom first... On the fire...

Terrible thing! Just terrible!

Her parents were beside themselves... Grease-stricken... (*Correcting himself.*) Grief... Grief-stricken...

Her father, the baron, developed an awful tic... (*He illustrates.*) He's never got rid of it...

Her mother just stood there, tearing her hair.

She's been bald ever since.

Anyway, as I was saying... That's the blemish... A scar...

But it's not just an ordinary, everyday scar.

Oh no.

You see, like everything else in their household, the frying-pan was embossed with the de Labelle crest... The family coat-of-arms...

So, now you understand. Ever since the accident, my fiancée—my Arabelle—has had two lions rampant, bar sinister, on her rump... And under them, the motto: "Honi Soit Qui Mal Y Pense!"

Terrible thing! Just terrible!

You'd think after all these years it would have faded. Skin, after all...

They tried everything, too.

But no use. It's still there.

And clearer than ever.

At least, that's what the baroness told me... I mean, I've really never seen it myself...

The crest... The inscription... And plain as day, the date: 1652.

That's right! Sixteen hundred and fifty-two!

A scar that old you don't get rid of overnight...

So there she is... My poor Arabelle... Disfigured for life...

Terrible thing! Just terrible!

But please, don't breathe a word. This is just between ourselves... If people hear she has a blemish, who knows what they might think? Some folks just love to imagine the worst!

There are even some men who wouldn't have her, I'm sure...

Just on account of a little thing like that.

Well, not me.

In fact, if you want to know the truth, that's why I decided to marry the young lady... Twenty-two years old, pretty, excellent character... Two hundred thousand francs...

Yes, I'm marrying her for her blemish.

I'm just crazy about antiques!

Besides, look at it this way: if she ever gets lost, they can find her in no time.

She's one of a kind.

No ifs, ands... Or buts...

Maurice Mac-Nab, *Une Tache*

Till Death Do Them Part

Dr. Joris A. Snowdrop, of Swineville, U.S.A., had arrived at the age of fifty-five, still a confirmed bachelor. Despite the urgings of relatives and friends, no one had been able to persuade him to take a wife.

Last year, however, a few days before Christmas, he found himself in his city's elegant Square Number Thirty-Seven, shopping for presents, and ventured into the vast emporium of Kitsch and Company, purveyors of plasticene *objets d'art*.

The person who waited on him was a young lady, large of stature and red of hair, who exuded such a wealth of charm that, for the first time in his life, the good doctor was smitten. When he went to pay he inquired who she was.

"Miss Bertha," was the reply.

And he promptly asked Miss Bertha if she would like to become his wife. Miss Bertha answered that she guessed she would like that fine. A fortnight after which, the ravishing Miss Bertha became Mrs. Joris A. Snowdrop, of Swineville, U.S.A.

For all his five and fifty summers the doctor was quite a presentable spouse. His boyish face was framed by fine silver locks, and he always took the greatest of care to keep it clean shaven.

He was, in a word, mad about his new young wife, indulging her every whim and lavishing upon her the most touching affection.

On his wedding-night, however, he had seen fit to advise her, in tones subdued but portentous:

"Bertha, my sweet… Should you ever decide to be unfaithful, please make sure I don't find out." Adding, a moment later: "For your own good, my precious…"

Now, it happened that Dr. Snowdrop, like many American physicians, had taken an apprentice, a medical student who followed him about on his rounds and attended his consultations. (An excellent practice, I might add, and one that might well teach our young French doctors to save more patients than they kill.)

At any rate, Dr. Snowdrop's apprentice—one George Arthurson by name—was a prettyish young man in his twenties, the son of one of his oldest and dearest friends, and the good doctor loved him like his own flesh and blood.

George, as it happened, was not at all immune to Miss Bertha's great beauty. But, upright to a fault, he kept his passion deep within his breast and flung himself headlong into his studies, to occupy his mind.

Miss Bertha, on the other hand, had loved George from the start; but, faithful wife that she was, she had resolved to wait and let him make the first move.

Such an impasse, clearly, was not destined to last. And, one fine day, George and Miss Bertha found themselves, indeed, wrapped in each other's arms.

George was utterly abashed at his weakness and swore he would never again let such a shameful thing take place. Miss Bertha, it seems, swore just the opposite.

The young man avoided her at every turn.

To no avail.

She plied him with letters fairly bursting with passion.

"Ah, George... To spend the rest of my life by your side... Never to be apart... My darling, if only our two beings might be merged into one, united and inseparable..."

The particular letter that contained that torrid effusion fell, by chance, into the hands of the good doctor, who muttered simply:

"As you wish, my sweet..."

That very evening they all dined at White Oak Park, one of the doctor's estates in the Swineville suburbs.

Gradually, as they ate, a strange irresistible torpor came over the two lovers.

With the help of Joe, a strapping old Black who had been in his employ since the War Between the States, Dr. Snowdrop undressed the adulterers, laid them out side by side, and anesthetized them by means of a hydrogen carbide preparation of his own invention.

He set about preparing his surgical instruments, so calmly, so methodically, that one would have thought he was about to do no more than cut off a Chinaman's bunion, or the like.

Then, with the most incredible skill, he proceeded to remove his wife's right arm and leg, severing them clearly and completely from her body.

Likewise the left arm and leg of young George.

Next, he stripped a three-inch-wide swath of skin down their respective sides.

After which, he placed the two bodies firmly against each other, taking care to match incision for incision, pressing them together and wrapping them tightly round, a good hundred times, with a long cloth bandage.

During the entire procedure, neither George nor Miss Bertha had so much as moved a muscle.

As soon as he was sure that their condition was stable, the doctor inserted a tube down his patients' gullets, into their stomachs, and began to feed them hot broth and a fine old bordeaux.

Thanks to his narcotic, administered in proper doses, the couple remained anesthetized for two full weeks.

On the first day of the third week he checked and satisfied himself that the healing was taking place according to schedule.

The incisions at the shoulders and thighs had scarred over.

The two sides had fused quite nicely into one.

It was then that Dr. Snowdrop's eyes flashed a look of triumph, and he discontinued the anesthetic.

George and Miss Bertha woke up together.

Quite.

At first, both assumed they were victims of some hideous, horrendous nightmare.

It was rather another matter when they realized it was no dream.

The good doctor looked on and couldn't hold back a smile.

As for the old Black, Joe, he could hardly contain himself.

The beautiful Miss Bertha seemed especially distraught, wailing and yelping like a mad hyena.

"Why, what ever is the matter?" Dr. Snowdrop cooed gently.

"I've only made your fondest wish come true, my precious... 'Ah, to spend the rest of my life by your side... Never to be apart... If only our two beings might be merged into one...'"

And, with a wry smile, he added:

"Some lovers do grow terribly attached to one another...'"

Alphonse Allais, *Collage*

A Lover's Cool Feat

He was waiting for her on the balcony, smoking cigarette after cigarette. It was cold. One of those frigid, brittle colds, dry as a bone... But so ebullient was he with the fever of expectation that the temperature scarcely mattered.

Finally a coach pulled up. A mass of black alighted against the pearl gray of the sidewalk, flashed by in an instant, and was swallowed up in the doorway.

Yes, it was she.

A trifle breathless from her headlong dash up two flights of stairs, she had no sooner entered than he began to plant voracious kisses over her sweet little hands and lovely large eyes.

Truly, she was a charming young thing, with a charm at once unforgettable and disquieting. Muffled up to her chin in furs, her pretty little head, with its brown locks and fine features, was wearing a boy's Tyrolean gray felt hat, brim pulled low over her brow. Those large eyes of hers seemed to be casting longer looks than was their wont; and she had, for the occasion, twirled those dainty ringlets about her temples—dubbed "beau-catchers" by some—but more elegant than any mere Spanish señorita's everyday little kiss-curls.

After the first effusive outpourings, unswathed and unswaddled, she observed somewhat sharply:

"Good Lord, my friend! It's like the North Pole in here!"

In desperation, he looked feverishly about for something to

burn. Some kind of fuel… Any kind… But alas, in vain…

Spending his life, as he did, out of doors, he had never considered that minor detail of domestic existence.

At which point, in a fit of truculent pique, she demanded:

"It's absurd, my friend! Burn your chairs, if you must… Anything… But for God's sake, make a fire! My feet are utterly frigid!"

That, however, he quite refused to do. His furniture had been his inheritance from his mother, and burning it struck him as repugnant and sacrilegious.

Rather, he hit on a compromise.

He invited her to take off her clothes and get into bed.

Himself, he stripped to the skin.

With a pocket knife that he first took care to sharpen, he made a neat incision the length of his belly, from his navel down, taking care not to cut too deeply.

She, somewhat perplexed, looked on with no notion whatever what he was about.

Then, suddenly understanding his plan, she burst out laughing and said, pleasantly as you please:

"Oh, my love! How terribly sweet!"

A moment later the operation was completed.

Clutching both hands to his protruding intestines, he crawled into bed.

She, not a little amused by it all, tucked her delicate pink feet into the iridescent mass of his fuming entrails, and uttered a little "oh" of surprise and delight.

Never had she imagined that it could be so warm in there.

He, for his part, suffered her frigid touch with agonizing distress. But the thought that she was comfortable assuaged him, and it was thus that they spent the night.

Though long since well warmed, she continued to lie there with her feet ensconced in her gallant beau's belly.

And it was truly an adorable sight to behold that pair of well-turned little feet, so elegantly arched, whose exquisite pink stood out all the more against the glaucous green of monsieur's bulging bowels.

Come morning, he was indeed a trifle fatigued, and even experienced some mild but annoying cramps.

But oh! How delightfully was he to be rewarded!

For she insisted on sewing back together, herself, that footmuff of flesh and blood.

And, like the nicest little homemaker, she went scurrying downstairs, in hatless haste, and purchased a fine steel needle and the loveliest green silk thread.

Then, with infinite precaution, her dainty left hand holding back his disgorging gut, with her dainty right she proceeded to sew up her selfless lover's wound.

Both would later agree that the memory of that night was their fondest of recollections.

Alphonse Allais, *Le Bon Amant*

Melt Down
or
The Case of the Migrating Petrolatum

Some people on this planet seem absolutely singled out for the most grotesque of adventures.

And the worst of it is that, rather than pity these wretched unfortunates, everyone, to a man, twits and chaffs them in their distress. (Or chaffs and twits, if you prefer.)

We need no better proof than the incredible communication that has just been handed me, from a reader of the Teutonic persuasion, and that I hasten to call to your attention. I quote...

(*Reading.*)

"*Mein lieber* and most esteemed monsieur,

"Please be so good as to permit one of your most devoted and long-time readers—though still a young man—to count on your boundless ingenuity and scientific knowledge to extricate him from a situation as painful as it is bizarre, and vice-versa.

"Mindful how valuable is every moment of your time, I shall state the facts directly with no further ado.

"Finding myself, the month of December last, in Vienna— the one on the Danube, not to be confused with your own little Vienne-on-the-Vienne—I fell in love with a certain Fraülein; not especially pretty, I must admit, but, as one of your modern novelists might put it, one whose figure's clean lines, fleshed out by exquisitely rotund attributes, titillated me *instanter*, and had soon captivated my heart, and all the rest.

"In no time I had married her.

"Cultivated and romantic dreamers that we were, we left at once to spend our honeymoon amid the Scandinavian fjords and the forests of Finland.

"That alone should suffice to assure you how little my dear Fraülein's aforementioned attributes had ceased to please me.

"But honeymoons, like the most agreeable of pleasantries, must sooner or later come to an end; and yesterday—yes, alas, my friend, yesterday—we alighted, my wife and I, here in Paris.

"Notwithstanding the heat wave that was searing your capital, we spent the whole day in long rambling strolls, and, in the evening, even faced the prospect of a doubtless torrid theater without the slightest trepidation.

"Oh, how quickly I came to regret that folly! For, already during the first *entr'acte* I noticed the face of my darling spouse—discomforted as she was, no doubt, by the heat—looking haggard and drawn; her features, indeed, beginning to stretch, to droop, as it were; such that, and so much that, by the end of the performance the poor child was utterly beyond all recognition.

"We hurried straight home.

"Much though she tried to resist, I made certain to remove her clothing myself.

"Ah, monsieur! If you could have seen!

"Her bosom, her glorious bosom, all gone!

"Her breasts, her magnificent breasts, like two biscuits!

"Her arms, her splendid arms, nothing but sticks!

"But as I continued to disrobe her my bewilderment grew all the greater.

"Her heavenly thighs, her flawless calves, her princessly ankles, her Cinderella feet… Good God, from the waist down, what a state she was in!

"Like the worst case of elephantiasis you can imagine!

"I thought I was dreaming!

"Embarrassed beyond words, fairly drowning awash in tears, my thenceforth monstrosity of a mate revealed to me the key to the riddle.

"Perhaps you recall, *mein lieber* and most esteemed monsieur, the recent innovation of a Viennese physician, reported in the press by one of your eminent journalistic confreres.

"Our Austrian savant had discovered a process by means of which to correct certain imperfections in the human figure, quite simply by injecting between the skin and flesh a quantity of petroleum jelly, or petrolatum, more or less, depending on the concavities to fill or the convexities to diminish.

"Pure petroleum jelly being a neutral and stable substance, resistant to putrefaction, its insertion into the human organism presents no danger whatever to the health of the individual thereby cosmetically retouched.

"All well and good, but a sport to be indulged in only in the winter!
"Because, God help us, in the summer?

"Calamity! Disaster! Ridicule heaped on shame!

"And so, esteemed monsieur and magnanimous mentor, I invoke the magnanimity of your genius… etc. etc…. your intellect…

etc. etc.... and beseech you... bla-bla-bla...

> Your obedient and faithful servant,
> Herr Thingum Von... Etc. etc."

To which I can only reply, *lieber* Herr Von Etcetera-Etcetera, that you really have only one last resort. Namely, to travel to the North Pole, both of you, and settle there for good.

Once there, you need merely, with sculptor's deft thumb, reshape you wife—remodel her, as it were—to suit you aesthetic taste.

Well now, if only that Viennese physician had thought to use Portland cement instead of petroleum jelly, we would never have to worry about such nasty little troubles.

Alphonse Allais, *La Fusible esthétique*

Split Decision
or,
The Blade, the Maid, and the Blade

They were walking together, the two of them, up the Avenue de l'Opéra.

He, a commonplace young blade, foppish to the hilt, in his shoes elegantly flat and pointed, his clothes modishly tight, which had doubtless cost him many a groan... In short, one of our blithe dimwit dandies: narrow silhouette and narrow mind to match.

She, on the other hand, a lovely little thing, pretty as a picture and petite as could be... A forehead run amuck with tight golden ringlets... But especially a figure!...

Incredible, that figure!...

A waist that our svelte little blonde could easily have belted with her bangle of massive gold...

So, there they were, walking up the Avenue de l'Opéra... He, with his flatfooted, dandified gait, witless blade that he was... She, sprightly of step, trotting along with her pert little head held high...

And behind them, a cavalry colossus who couldn't believe what he saw...

Transfixed, utterly, by the sight of that hourglass figure, Paris-style, and comparing it in his mind's eye to his own buxom lovely's far more generous girth, he kept muttering to himself:

"It can't be real... It's a fake... It's a fake..."

A ridiculous supposition, obviously, for anyone who has studied even the most modest smattering of anatomy...

One can, to be sure, have false teeth, wigs and wiglets, added hips and padded bosoms. But by no stretch of the imagination can one conceive of an artificial waist.

Still, our dragoon—a mere private, as it happened—was as ill informed on matters anatomical as on vestimental and such like deceptions, and kept muttering, aghast:

"It's a fake... It's a fake..."

By now they had arrived at the outer boulevard.

The couple turned right and, though it wasn't his direction, the dragoon did likewise and kept following behind.

No, certainly not, it just wasn't possible... That waist couldn't be a real one... And, calling to mind his village's most striking belles, try as he might he couldn't remember a single one as slender, even remotely, as this incredibly, unthinkably wasp-waisted beauty...

As length our dubious and disturbed hussar decided to find out once and for all, and muttered:

"Well, we'll just see if it's real or not."

And, stepping up two paces to the young woman's right, he unsheathed his sword.

Suddenly the flat broad blade whished in a horizontal arc and sliced her—like the earthworm severed by the gardener's cruel hoe—into two neat portions that went rolling along the pavement.

Our other blade stood making rather a nasty face, if you can imagine…

Alphonse Allais, *Pour en avoir le cœur net*

Dressing to Kill

I don't know if you feel the way I do, but it seems to me that good help should never be mistreated. Not even a little.

When you realize that, for a pittance, these folk devote themselves, day in day out, you have to admit that we do get our money's worth. No need to go adding nasty epithets in the bargain, or offensive gestures.

Besides, you'd better keep in mind that servants aren't quick to forget a grudge, and that they have an amazing talent for getting even when they have to.

For example, let me tell you about the delicious little joke that a cook who worked for a woman I heard of played... A friend of mine... (The cook, that is...) Anyway, her name was Clémentine and she worked for the woman and her husband. Stupid, carping people, both of them.

Now, Clémentine was a superb cook. She knew her business from A to Z, and she practiced it with impeccable good taste, never letting her tempestuous, romantic nature get out of hand.

Her employers were a *nouveau riche* couple, definitely lower class, who had made their fortune in some shady little trade or other. Which didn't keep them from putting on airs. Far from it. The wife especially. Infuriatingly so.

"Clémentine!" she would screech. "You've absolutely ruined your veal marengo!"

And Clémentine would just keep quiet and shrug it off.

"Clémentine!" the battleaxe would hound her. "Your mutton is vile! It's nothing but grease!"

And the same reaction from Clémentine. That is, none at all.

One day it was the salad's turn to be reviled by the old harpie:

"Clémentine!" she squealed. "What kind of foul dressing did you put on this salad? Kerosene?"

From that moment on, it was one never-ending invective against poor Clémentine's salad.

Madame even insisted on personally buying the ingredients. The very best oil. The very best vinegar.

But the salad was no better.

No doubt it was Clémentine's proportions... Not enough vinegar... Too much oil...

Or vice-versa.

And so, finally, she decided to make the salad herself.

It just so happened that, at the time, Clementine had a lover. A bright little young man who worked in a chemistry laboratory at the Collège de France.

Informed of the tribulations his ladyfriend was being made to suffer, the bright little young man asked her:

"Would you like a good laugh?"

"I'd love one," she replied.

"Fine!… Then I'll bring you some oil and vinegar of my own. Just be sure they get used the next time those two baboons give a fancy dinner…"

And, true to his word, the bright little young man brought her his oil and vinegar. Only the "vinegar" was a mixture of sulphuric and nitric acids. And the "oil" was a high grade of glycerine, slightly yellow in color.

Now, any of you who have spent as little as two or three months in a dynamite factory are aware that the aforementioned substances, when mixed together, make up what is conventionally known as nitroglycerine.

When the mixture is suddenly and carelessly disturbed, the result is a rise in temperature, followed by one of those explosions that leave you no choice but to cash in your chips. If you can find them, that is.

Well, things happened as planned.

Despite the pomp and circumstance of the dinner that evening, Madame simply insisted on preparing the salad herself. In due course the salad bowl exploded to bits and all the guests were showered with a violent barrage of chicory.

Unfortunately, the accident didn't quite stop there.

The dishes and glasses went shattering to pieces too. Likewise the table. As well as the faces, and the arms, and the legs of all the fine ladies and gentlemen in attendance.

Meanwhile, there were two people in the kitchen, laughing their heads off.

Alphonse Allais, *Farce légitime*

To Break a Bed Habit

Little Mimi Doré might well have been the most exquisite young woman of her time, were it not for one flaw.

Mademoiselle Doré, Mimi, was by far the soul of infidelity, you see. Oh là là, the very soul... She would cheat on her lovers without batting an eye. Or, for that matter, sometimes batting either one, or both.

At the time our tale begins, Mimi's lover *pro tem* was a certain Monsieur Jacques (of Jacques and Gilles, Ltd.), a promising young magnate on his way to the top, destined for the high-water mark of Parisian entrepreneurship.

But while on his way up, as it were, the young Monsieur Jacques—a pale, fetching fellow—fell (nay, tumbled) in love with the faithless Mimi.

Head over heels.

Now, the first time Monsieur Jacques caught Mimi cheating, he asked her:

"But why? Why with him?"

"Because he's handsome," was her reply.

"I see," he muttered.

O omnipotence of love! O triumph of the will! When Monsieur Jacques returned that evening, he was utterly transformed.

No longer pale, he was ruddy and radiant. No longer merely fetching, he was handsome beyond belief. Next to him, Adonis himself would have faded into insignificance.

The second time Monsieur Jacques caught Mimi cheating, he asked her:

"But why? Why with him?"

"Because he's rich," was her reply.

"I see," he muttered.

And that very day, he invented a process, with a minimum investment of time and labor, for turning horse droppings into lavender plush.

The Americans fought over the patent with fistfuls of dollars. Even fistfuls of "eagles"... A bird in the hand, so to speak... (Oh, in case you don't know, the "eagle" is a twenty-dollar gold piece, worth one hundred four francs, thirty centimes, at the present exchange rate.)

The third time Monsieur Jacques caught Mimi cheating, he asked her:

"But why? Why with him?"

"Because he's funny," was her reply.

"I see," he muttered.

And he hurried to the bookstore, where he purchased a collection of uproarious stories.

He read and re-read the hilarious volume from cover to cover, and learned it so well that Mimi, that night, nearly split her sides laughing.

The fourth time Monsieur Jacques caught Mimi cheating, he asked her:

"But why? Why with him?"

"Because he... Because his... Because he has a... a... You know!" was her reply.

Now, if this were a pornographic tale, which I rather wish it were, I fancy you might enjoy hearing the extensive measures he undertook forthwith.

The fifth time Monsieur Jacques caught Mimi cheating...

Damn! Really, at this rate...

The one thousand one hundred fourteenth time Monsieur Jacques caught Mimi cheating, he asked her:

"But why? Why with him?"

"Because he's a killer," was her reply.

"I see," he muttered.

And Monsieur Jacques proceeded to kill Mademoiselle Mimi.

It was at that time, roughly, that she lost her taste for cheating on Monsieur Jacques.

Alphonse Allais, *Comme les autres*

Just for Malpractice

Too much studying can be dangerous. Even downright deadly...

I knew a really serious student once. A law student. At least, that's what he was supposed to be. Actually, what he was studying was medicine. Law? Not a word!... That's how it is with some really serious students.

Anyway, as I was saying, medicine was his passion. Day in, day out, his nose was always in the books. Nothing else in life mattered. It was the only thing he knew. Ask him to be a fourth at bridge, for example, and he'd have to be the dummy. I'm telling you... A dummy at everything, in fact! Take my word! And especially when it came to women...

That's why a few of us just couldn't resist... We invited him to come to dinner one night, and took bets to see how he'd act. He accepted, but only on one condition. That we let him do the carving. He said it would give him good practice for doing dissections!... Now do you believe me?

Well, first we thought we should get him relaxed. So, before we sat down, we gave him a shot of absinth. Then some rum to help it down... And some crème de menthe for a chaser... And a big glass of punch to get rid of the taste of the crème de menthe... And another shot of absinth to top it all off...

At dinner you can guess where we put him, I'm sure... Right! Next to a beautiful, sweet, young thing... Not the brightest in the world, but built like a... Well... Built! From every direction... Top, bottom, and in between... Solid as the Sorbonne...

The effect was tremendous. Our friend didn't take a mouthful. He just sat there staring, and mumbling things like: "Ah! Lovely maxilla!... Beautiful scapula!... Exquisite ulna!... Stunning patella!..." The sweet young thing was terribly offended. "Are you going to keep talking about all your girl friends?" she pouted.

But when all was said and done, the two of them left together.

★

Next morning, my friends and I decide to pay him a visit. Not too early... His first time, after all... So we wait until ten. Then we tiptoe up the stairs...

When we get to his room, we see the key is in the door... We open it and go in, humming a serenade...

We took one look and... Good God! It was horrible!... The sweet young thing was still there, all right... In a manner of speaking... At least, all the pieces...

Léon Xanrof, *L'Amour de l'étude*

Ethnic Cleansing 1900:
A Fool and His Mania
or
Dyeing Can Be Fatal

One day I got a letter from Timbuctou. It was from a friend of mine who was writing to say hello, and to tell me about some strapping Sudanese or other who was going to be coming to pay me a visit. "He'll be happy to hire himself out," he assured me. "And besides, it won't cost you a thing if you just give him room and board. All he wants is a chance to spend some time in Paris."

"Free help!" I said to myself. "Damn! I'll say!..." So I waited for his Sudanese.

One morning the bell rang. When I opened the door, there was this character standing in front of me, with a face as black as pitch... But I mean black! I'm telling you, so black that I almost panicked... He was holding out his hand with a letter. In my friend's handwriting...

"Aha!" I said. "You must be that Sudanese."

"Oui, m'sié, he answered.

"But my dear chap," I muttered, "what happened? You're a sight!"

I motioned him inside. He stood staring at me, blankly.

"Come on... Come get yourself cleaned up!" I insisted. "Why, you're absolutely black!"

"Oui, m'sié. Me black," he nodded.

I must say he didn't seem too terribly concerned. So I pulled him over and stood him in front of a mirror.

"Just look at yourself," I said. "You poor thing! What the devil have you been poking your nose into, to get so black!"

"Oui, m'sié. Me black," he repeated.

And he just kept smiling, flashing a mouthful of gleaming white teeth. I couldn't help wondering how anyone so careful to keep his teeth that clean could possibly go and let his face get that dirty. So I asked him again what in heaven's name had happened. How on earth had he managed to let it get so black... "Is it ink?" I asked him? "Is it soot?... Coal?... Tar?..." Obviously he had no idea what I was saying.

"Here... Get undressed," I told him, and I went to heat up some water. "May as well give the poor thing a bath," I thought... Well, when I saw him without a stitch I couldn't believe my eyes! Damned if he wasn't just as black all over! I mean, not only his face and his hands... His whole body! Every inch!... You can't imagine! He couldn't have had a bath in the last twenty years!... So I asked him again. But I still couldn't get a word out of him! Not a word, I'm telling you!... Really, he had to be a little soft in the head or something!

Anyway, I got him into the tub and began soaping him up and scrubbing as hard as I could. But it wouldn't come off... Not the least little bit. Still I kept scrubbing. Harder and harder... I'm not one to give up, believe me!... Well, after five minutes I realized that soap wasn't going to work, and that I'd have to try something else.

I thought maybe if I scraped him with a knife... To see if I could get the bulk of it off at least... But you should have heard him howl! That really began to get me discouraged, and I wondered if I shouldn't just let him wallow in his filth... "But no," I said to myself. "I can't. It's not right to leave any human being to suffer in such a state!..." No, it was my duty, plain and simple, to try to get him clean. So I did my best. I rubbed him with a file... With pumice... With bleach water mixed with lye... Useless, every one of them! But I didn't give up. His skin was beginning to chap and crack all over. "Aha! At last a little progress!" I thought. "Now if only I can find the right detergent..." And I tried. I experimented with this and that... With

every kind I could think of... Benzine, kerosene, ammonia, turpentine... One after another, they took turns on his epidermis. Every night I came home with some new concoction. As soon as he heard me he would run and try to hide. But I would always find him and begin again... And again, and again... And each time I scrubbed him, each time I scoured and scraped, he would look up at me with such a pitiful hangdog look and give out with such pathetic groans... It was enough to break your heart, believe me. I had all I could do not to burst into tears. And more than once too... But I couldn't let sentiment keep me from my duty. I kept telling myself that this poor soul's well-being was all that really mattered... That it was worth a few passing moments of excruciating pain, and that he would be the first, in the long run, to thank me... Soon his body was one big festering blister.

One night, when I went to bathe him, I heated up the water hotter than you can imagine. His sores were something awful... I rubbed him with sandpaper. Blood came spurting out everywhere... I scraped him with chips of broken glass... Still nothing, no improvement! He just looked like a skinned rabbit.

I finally realized it was no use, and that I could never get him clean. I'd have to try something else. And I said to myself: "Look, when a building is covered with grime, what's the best way to fix it up? Not to stand around trying to scrape off each smudge, one by one... No, they paint over it." And then and there I decided: "I'll paint my Sudanese white, that's what!"

So I bought a lot of white greasepaint and set to work smearing it all over him. When he looked at himself and saw that he was white from head to toe, you can't imagine his delight! He went prancing about and posing in front of every mirror in the flat.

"Oh, you good boss!" he said again and again. "Me pretty, pretty, pretty!"

Well, me good boss all right, considering all the pains I was going to for this creature's personal hygiene! But him pretty, pretty, pretty...? That's another matter! Frankly, he looked like a clown.

And a sick one at that... But at least he was looking clean... More or less... I was finally getting somewhere.

Now, I don't know if it was because the greasepaint was cracking, or because the dust in my flat was beginning to cover it. But after a few days dark splotches began to show here and there. Soon my Sudanese was a cross between a checkerboard and a patchwork quilt.

Then, little by little, the two colors began to blend. His body was nothing but an ugly grayish mass, more disgusting to look at now than the black he started out with.

"No," I said to myself. "It's obvious that the white paint is never going to stick." And I thought: "Let's see now... Maybe what I need is some primer... Like when they paint the metal grilles on windows and things... First red, then whatever... Yes, that's what I'll do. I'll give him a few good undercoats first."

So I got some iron oxide paint and spread it on, nice and even... And thick... I must say, I enjoyed it. I suddenly understood why children love their paint sets so much! Great fun, really...

When he saw himself all red, from head to toe, my Sudanese couldn't have been more pleased. He went jumping up and down. Once his head almost hit the ceiling...

"Oh, you good boss!" he kept saying. "Me pretty, pretty, pretty!"

But the next day he complained that he itched all over. The second day he said that his skin was on fire. The third, his cries and shrieks filled the flat. I told him to try to be patient... After all, we had already come a long way. It was clear that we were making progress... I promised that he wouldn't have to put up with the pain much longer. That shut him up, thank goodness.

Once the primer was good and dry I gave him a coat of pearl gray paint. I rather liked the shade. It seemed to me a big step closer to white.

Well, when he saw that he was pearl gray now, from head to toe, he was absolutely ecstatic. Myself, frankly, I was almost as pleased. You can't imagine how beautiful a pearl gray body looks until you've seen one. Some Sunday, if you have nothing else to do... Try it. Really, it's very chic. You'll see...

It was just then that I had to leave on a little trip. So I took a sheet of paper, wrote WET PAINT, and stuck it to my Sudanese's back.

When I came home a few days later he was in bed.

I don't know if it was the red paint, or the gray, or maybe both. But the fact is his skin was burning up. Why, I can't imagine.. What's worse, the color was beginning to disappear in spots... His back and his buttocks were almost completely black. From rubbing against the bed, I suppose... His belly was reddish. His face, a kind of gray... His arms and legs, an off-white... More or less... Not to mention the thousands of shades in between! I had never seen so many, believe me!

I realized finally that, no matter how hard I tried, paint just wasn't going to work, I'd have to try something else.

"Why not gold leaf?" I asked myself.

And I bought a barrelful of it. It cost me a fortune, let me tell you. But I'm not one to shrink from any expense where my fellow man's comfort and well-being are concerned, I assure you!

Anyway, when he saw that he was a glittering mass of gold, from head to toe, he was absolutely delirious.

"Me rich! Me rich!" he cackled. And he went flouncing about the flat with glee.

It seems the two of us could be seen from the street, because in no time a pair of gendarmes came knocking at the door and insisted on speaking with me. When I hurried to see what our fine public servants could possibly have in mind, they accused me of stealing the statue from the Place de la Bastille, if you can imagine!... Well, I suggested that, before they hung such a heinous crime on me, if you please, they would do well to find out if it had actually been committed! One of them said that, yes, he would go look, and the other one would stay and make sure that I didn't escape.

Meanwhile my Sudanese just kept dancing for joy from mirror to mirror.

"Me rich! Me rich! he exulted.

Him rich, for sure... But when two weeks went by I noticed that his wealth was beginning to drop off... Literally, I mean... There were little flakes everywhere. On the furniture, on the floor... I had thought about appointing someone with power of attorney, to manage his fortune for him. But at the rate he was losing it... Well, by time the legal formalities were taken care of, there wouldn't be any left!

Clearly it was time to try something else. This is how I saw the situation:

"Paints don't last, and gold leaf is no better. There's only one solution: I'll have to nickel-plate him."

So I plunged him, head to toe, into an electroplating bath. After some fifteen minutes, when he didn't seem to be moving, I asked him how he felt. He didn't answer, so I reached in and pulled him out. I must say, he'd grown terribly heavy...

I set him down in front of me. He didn't budge. A trifle concerned, I took his arm and gave it a little shake. But his whole body moved, like a single, solid block. Which is what, in fact, he was... His feet gave a hollow, metallic sound against the floor. I went to feel his pulse... He didn't have one. He was dead.

Since then I've fitted him with a figleaf and I've been using him as a doorstop...

Edouard Osmont, *Mon nègre*

To Serve One's Fellows
or
A Ship of Foods

A stroll by the seashore is no idle waste of time. As proof, witness the documents I am about to read to you, and which I found the other day in a bottle just as the surf that had brought it in was quickly pulling back—not, I imagine, in horror and disgust, though one might be tempted to conjecture as much, but simply because the tide had turned and was on its way out.

Let me share with you the most interesting fragment of what must, apparently, have been a ship's log.

(*Reading.*)

"April 17. It has been exactly one month today since our vessel began to drift. And in all this time not another human soul have we encountered! It is amazing how barren the Atlantic can be this time of year. Not a single shore. We might as well have deaf-mutes in the crow's nest! All of our provisions are exhausted, alas! Meeting at noon tomorrow, on deck, to draw lots.

"April 18. We are all up on deck. The captain has a number of little slips of paper in his cap. Earlier, it was the Dutch merchant who broke the silence. 'Who knows, my dear friends,' he said, 'but what four or five weeks from now we may not come upon another vessel? Why sacrifice human lives until all hope is lost? It is best, I think, that we proceed more slowly. Piecemeal, one might say. Let us, rather, cut off one by one—as the need arises, and by lot—first the left legs of all the passengers and crew. Then likewise all the right legs; and, should our distress continue, all the arms, left then right. Needless to say, the surgeon will be exempted, as well as the cook.'

"The proposal has been accepted in principle, though not without much interesting discussion. The professor amongst us—the biologist—has assured us that a man of average stature, by dining on his arms and legs—previously cooked or salted, to be sure—could comfortably exist for about one hundred ten days. 'According to that calculation,' he added, 'however many of us there may be on board, we shall each nonetheless be able to survive one hundred ten days on our communal edibles—our arms and legs, that is. Now I ask you, would we not be better advised to cut them all off presently, all at once, rather that later, a few at a time? We grow thinner by the day. Never will they be as "corpulent," so to speak, as they are at this moment. Furthermore, bodies with neither arms nor legs have substantially less flesh, and therefore require less nourishment to sustain them.'

"The learned scientist's opinion was not shared by the government magistrate on board. 'Imagine,' said the latter, 'should we shortly happen upon another vessel, how bitter would be our regret at having cut off one hundred fifty arms and legs for no reason whatever. What will we do with all that useless larder? No charities, I venture, will accept it. Even the prisons will refuse to take it off our hands, so to speak.'

"The judge's opinion has prevailed. Tonight the surgeon will set about his task. Namely, the amputation of the first three left legs, properly sterilized and bandaged, belonging respectively to one of the crew, a wench of dubious virtue, and a Japanese army officer.

"May 18. Obviously that English Lady So-and-So wasn't nearly so slim as her corsets made her appear. We all made quite a respectable meal of her left calf, and there remains a good helping of foot on ice for tomorrow morning's breakfast.

"June 17. It is curious how many legless individuals one sees squatting about the deck of late.

"July 14. Bastille Day. A gala dinner planned for this evening. A special dish for the occasion. The first mate's arm on a fish platter with two beautiful flags tattooed on the inside of his forearm…"

⭐

That's as much as I've been able to decipher so far... What ever became of that ship, I wonder? If it does manage to reach port safely all you circus owners and carnival hucksters had better take note! There's bound to be a major drop in the going rate for human torsos. A veritable glut on the market, so to speak...

Tristan Bernard, *Cannibalisme*

Of Arms—Eyes, Mouths, Noses—
and the Man

On my last trip to Alaska I was most warmly received by a delegation from the League for Eugenics, whose directress—a particularly beautiful young miss, I must say—immediately spoke to me as follows:

"Please do not imagine, monsieur, that our organization's sole purpose is the genetic improvement of the human species. We aim no less at developing the individual once he has come into the world, and at perfecting his physical endowments, so to speak, for life. It is our intention, therefore, to devote our energies, to the fullest, to expanding that new branch of medical science know as "cosmetic surgery." Its progress and innovations, which we follow with keen interest, have already been considerable. With a zeal and determination typical of the young race that peoples these climes, and whom you come to study, our cosmetic surgeons are expanding the frontiers of their specialty and its objectives in a manner which your own practitioners, I daresay, have not yet even imagined. It is quite incredible. Come back tomorrow morning, monsieur, at nine o'clock. I shall be happy to have you visit our clinic and show you the quality of work we are doing there. You will be able to see for yourself the gratifying results that we have already obtained."

So saying, the charming creature gave a faint little nod. That was that: our chat was concluded. And off she scurried, flitting lightly as a dragonfly while telephones tinkled their bells in every corner of the elegant establishment.

Next morning I arrived quite punctually and was taken at once to what the directress called her "laboratory," and where she expounded her ideas concerning the improvement of the human species. That done, she ushered me into another room, occupied by a rather good-looking young man.

With a gesture in his direction she explained:

"Monsieur is from Switzerland. He lost an arm in a railroad accident. Our surgeons have replaced it with the arm of an ape, modified appropriately in appearance. First, by peeling off the skin little by little, and then, as each site scarred over, by grafting strips of the patient's own skin in its place. It is, of course, a slow and painstaking procedure, given the extreme care and precaution that such an operation demands if it is to be successful. Still, difficult as it is, it pales when compared to the other operation that monsieur has undergone—with admirable courage, I might add—and which has been a complete and total success.

And, addressing the young man, she continued:

"Please turn around, monsieur, and let him see."

He did. And I saw that, set just above his left ear, he had an eye. It was looking at me. In back of his head he had another, which was observing me as well. And, above his right ear, a third eye—or fifth one, to be precise. I was, need I say, quite startled.

"Monsieur," explained my hostess, is a supervisor in a very large factory by profession. We felt that his two normal eyes were inadequate for a task that required the ability to see on all sides at once. That being the case, our surgeons, whose skill is quite extraordinary, have given him three additional eyes, and have transformed him into a veritable Argos... I assume you recall your Greek mythology, monsieur... At any rate, he could not be more delighted, since a five-eyed supervisor commands a rather substantial salary."

I was so astonished that I stood there, speechless. But a moment later we left and went into an adjoining room, where I was introduced to another gentleman.

"Permit me to present our most distinguished politician, the mayor of Dawson City."

"Delighted," I replied.

"His Honor was married not long ago, and, in a fit of rage his wife bit off his nose. Our surgeons have given him a new one even nicer than the first, carved out of a rabbit's backside. While they were at it—and with his consent, of course—they decided to give him another mouth as well, fully equipped with all the necessary parts. I'll not trouble you with the details of that delicate operation. Suffice it to say that His Honor is now able to speak out of both his mouths at once."

The distinguished politician obligingly turned round, and I saw, at the base of his neatly shaven skull, a perfectly shaped mouth. He was more than willing at my beaming hostess's request, to recite two poems at once by way of demonstration. While his natural mouth held forth with the beginning of Canto One of *Paradise Lost*, the new one, in an almost unaccented French—in deference to myself, no doubt—declaimed a celebrated soliloquy from Racine's *Phèdre*.

I was, of course, stunned.

"You can appreciate," my guide was quick to explain, "the importance that a second mouth can have for a politician. His Honor can now express himself with the utmost clarity, out of doors as well as in, not only to those listening in front of him, but also to those behind. I needn't emphasize," she concluded, "the advantages that a second orifice of this kind presents."

"One would think," I remarked as we took our leave of the distinguished politician, "that you were, as you suggest, inspired by the ancient myths, with their characters sporting many a this and that... Many eyes, many mouths..."

"Yes," replied the lovely directress of the League for Eugenics. "And many arms as well. No doubt you remember Briareos, in the *Iliad*."

"No doubt," I nodded.

"Well," she continued, showing me to the next room, "we have here his incarnation…"

I entered and saw a man with four arms.

"Our friend is an officer of the law. He came to us of his own accord and asked us to give him a few more arms, in the hope that he might become even more formidable to the rabble than he already was. As you see, we have obliged him admirably. Since he is a gentleman of unusual strength, now that he has four arms, including this one on his stomach and that one on his back, he will be able to arrest four felons at once, and, single-handedly—or so to speak—haul them to the police station."

She made her exit amid a flurry of my copious congratulations, telling me that she was off to attend a most delicate surgical procedure. It was to be performed upon an eminent scientist who, in order to examine the natural world in more thorough detail, had asked to have eyes grafted onto his fingertips… Tiny eyes, to be sure… A hummingbird's eyes… So as not to interfere in the slightest with his sense of touch.

I left the laboratory and immediately put pen to paper in order to record the curious cases I have observed. I am certain that our age will provide these surgical cosmeticians with opportunities to apply their theories and skills in most unforeseen ways and, doubtless, to the excellent advantage of the human species.

Guillaume Apollinaire, *Chirurgie esthétique*

The Disappearance of Honoré Subrac
or
Point Blank

Despite the most thorough and painstaking investigation, the police have been unable to shed any light on the mysterious disappearance of Honoré Subrac.

Since he was my friend, however, and seeing that I knew precisely what had happened, I felt it was my duty to inform the authorities. The magistrate who took my statement listened to me dutifully and wrote down every word. But when I was through, it was clear from his tone of exaggerated politeness that he thought—and rather uneasily—that I must be a lunatic. I called this to his attention, but it only succeeded in making him treat me even more politely... Finally he stood up and urged me toward the door. His bailiff, I noticed, was standing there at the ready, fists clenched, about to pounce in case I became violent.

I thought it best not to insist. The case of Honoré Subrac, after all, is so utterly bizarre that the truth itself is quite beyond belief. No doubt you recall from the newspaper accounts that he was something of an eccentric, dressing as he did in nothing but a greatcoat, and with only slippers on his feet. He was, however, a very wealthy man. And since I too found his costume rather curious, to say the least, I asked him one day to explain the reason for it.

"To get out of it quickly if I have to," was his reply. "It's easy," he continued, "to get used to going about without very much on. We really don't need underwear, or stockings, or a hat... Why, I've been dressing this way since I was twenty-five, and I've never been sick a day..."

Rather than clarify matters for me, his words only made me all the more curious.

"Why on earth should he have to undress so fast?" I mused.

And my mind came up with a number of explanations...

★

Now then, one night, as I was on my way home—it may have been one o'clock, or even a quarter after—I heard someone call out my name in a whisper. It seemed to be coming from the wall, right beside me, just as I was passing... I stopped in surprise, and somewhat annoyed.

"We're quite alone, aren't we? murmured the voice. "It's me... Honoré Subrac..."

"But where the devil are you?" I shouted, looking all around, unable to imagine where my friend could be hiding.

All I saw was that famous greatcoat of his, lying on the ground, and, beside it, his no-less-celebrated slippers.

"Aha!" I said to myself. "Obviously this is one of those moments when he had to undress in a hurry! At last I'm going to get to the bottom of this mystery..."

And I said, out loud:

"It's all right, old man. We're alone. You can come out..."

All at once, there was Honoré Subrac, emerging somehow from against the wall, where only a moment before I had failed to see him. He was naked from head to toe. Snatching up his greatcoat, he wrapped himself round and buttoned it up as fast as he could. Then he put on his slippers and walked with me to my door.

"I surprised you, didn't I!" he said, in a perfectly natural tone of voice. "Well, maybe now you can see why I have to dress so oddly. Though I daresay you still don't have the faintest idea why you couldn't see me there... But really, it's quite simple. A case of protective coloration, that's all... Mother Nature is very kind. She gives those of

148

her children who are weak and defenseless the gift of blending in with their surroundings. But I'm sure you know all that… That butterflies, for example, look like flowers, and certain insects, like leaves… That the chameleon can take on the color that hides it best… Or that the Arctic hare turns white as the snow, and, as timid as our own, can scurry across the frozen wastes, almost invisible…

"Yes," he continued, "powerless though they are, some animals foil their enemies with this inborn ability to change their appearance. As for me," he explained, "pursued as I am by a relentless enemy, too fearful and weak to defend myself… Yes, I too share their gift. To put it simply, when I'm frightened I can blend in with the scenery.

"I first discovered that I had this gift a number of years ago. I was twenty-five at the time, and women—at least most of them—found me pleasant and rather attractive. One of them, in fact, a married lady, made such a show of affection that I really couldn't resist!… One night, I was with my new mistress, at her home. Her husband had supposedly gone away for a few days. The two of us were naked as the day we were born, when all of a sudden the door flew open and there he stood, brandishing a revolver… I was terrified! Coward that I was—and am—I had only one thought in mind: to vanish on the spot!… As I backed against the wall, I wished with all my might that I could disappear into the woodwork. And, much to my amazement, that's exactly what happened. In a manner of speaking… In a word, I turned the precise color of the wallpaper. At the same time, my arms and legs, in an incomprehensible effort of will, spread flat against the wall until it seemed that I was actually part of it, and that no one, from that moment on, could see me. In fact, that was the case. The husband kept looking, high and low, to kill me. He had seen me, and he knew that I couldn't possibly have escaped… In a fit of fury, he turned savagely on his wife, shooting her dead with six bullets in the brain. Then, whimpering in despair, he left… As soon as he was gone, my body, instinctively, returned to its normal color and shape. I got dressed and ran out before anyone else arrived…

"This fortunate talent for protective coloration has been with me ever since. The poor lady's husband, unable to kill me then and there, has devoted his life to pursuing that end, dogging my tracks far and wide for all these years. When I came here to live in Paris I

thought at last I would be rid of him... But no!... Just now, I saw him... A moment before you came by, there he was! Terror gripped me... My teeth began to chatter... I only had time to throw off my clothes and melt against the wall. He passed right beside me, and gave a curious look at my greatcoat and slippers lying there on the side-walk... And so, now you can see, I'm sure, why I'm right to dress so lightly! My gift would be useless if I wore clothes like the rest of you. I could never get them off fast enough to escape, don't you under-stand? I've got to be naked. Otherwise, my clothes, spread out against the wall, would give me away, disappearance notwithstanding..."

I congratulated Subrac on possessing an ability that I myself had seen proven before my very eyes, and one that I frankly envied...

For the next few days I thought of nothing else. I would catch myself, from time to time, straining with all my might to alter my shape and color. I tried and tried to will myself into a bus... The Eiffel Tower... A member of the Académie Française... A grand prize win-ner in the national lottery... But to no avail. As hard as I tried, it was simply beyond me. My will wasn't strong enough. And besides, what I lacked above all was that unholy terror, that sense of imminent cata-strophic doom that had first aroused the instinct of Honoré Subrac...

I hadn't seen my friend for quite some time when, one day, suddenly, he appeared in sheer panic.

"He's after me!" he cried. "That man... The husband... The one who wants to kill me... Everywhere I go... I've disappeared three times, but I don't know how much longer... I'm afraid, my friend... Afraid... Afraid..."

I noticed, indeed, how emaciated he had become, but I was careful not to tell him.

"There's only one solution," I answered. "If you want to

escape him you've got to run away. Go find yourself some little village to hide in. Don't worry, I'll stay and take care of your affairs. You just leave! Anywhere! And from the nearest station, understand?..."

He seized my hand in his and said: "Please! I'm afraid!... Come with me! Please..."

★

We walked along in silence. Honoré Subrac kept looking back anxiously over his shoulder... All of a sudden he let out a scream and broke away like a shot, throwing off his greatcoat and slippers as he ran. I turned around to look. Yes, there was a man, lurching wildly toward us. I tried to stop him. He pushed me aside... He was holding a revolver and was aiming it straight at Honoré Subrac... My friend had just managed to reach the edge of a long barracks wall, and vanished as if by magic.

The man with the revolver stopped short in consternation, bellowing with rage. As if to wreak vengeance on the wall that had deprived him, seemingly, of his prey, he fired point blank at the spot were Honoré Subrac had disappeared. Then he went running off...

A crowd began to gather. The police came and dispersed it. I called to my friend, but there was no answer.

Then I touched the wall. It still felt warm. And I noticed that, of the six bullets fired, three had hit the wall at the height of a man's heart. The others had crumbled the plaster a little higher up, where I thought I could make out, vaguely, the shape of a human face...

Guillaume Apollinaire, *La Disparition d'Honoré Subrac*

Ahead and Behind

I had a friend once, a Swiss fellow, Hans Bonkers by name. He was living in Peru, twelve thousand feet up. He had gone there exploring a few years before, and had lost his heart to the charms of a strange Indian woman, who had driven him utterly out of his mind with love unrequited. Little by little he had begun to waste away until, finally, he was too weak even to leave his cabin. A Peruvian doctor who had accompanied him on his travels treated him as best he could for a *dementia præcox*, which he felt, however, to be quite incurable.

One night, a sudden influenza epidemic struck the little Indian village where Hans Bonkers was being cared for. Every one of the natives contracted the disease, without exception. In a few days, of the original two hundred, one hundred seventy-eight were dead. In a panic, the Peruvian doctor hurried back to Lima... My friend, stricken like all the rest, lay languishing with fever.

Now, it happened that all of the Indians had one or more dogs, who soon had no choice, if they were to survive, but to eat their dead masters. And so they proceeded to dismember their cadavers. One of them came trotting into Hans Bonkers' hut, carrying in its mouth the head of the Indian woman he adored... He recognized it at once. The shock, I imagine, was so intense that it jarred him back to his senses, curing him of both his fever and his madness. He took the head in his hands and, with renewed vigor, playfully threw it across the room, telling the dog to "go fetch!" Once, twice, three times... And the beast would dutifully retrieve it, clutching it by the nose, in its teeth.

But the third time Hans Bonkers bowled a little too hard, and the head smashed against the wall. As the brain rolled out he was delighted to observe that it consisted of two smooth, rounded hemispheres, that looked for all the world like a pair of firm buttocks...

Francis Picabia,
"*Entr'acte de cinq minutes,*" from *Jésus-Christ rastaquouère.*

The Debutante

or

Defaced

When I was a girl, I went to the zoo a lot. I went so often that I got to know the animals better than other young ladies my age. Every day, in fact, as a kind of escape. The animal I got to know best was a young girl hyena. She knew me too. She was terribly bright. I gave her French lessons and she taught me hyena language. That way we spent lots of pleasant hours together.

My mother was arranging my debutante party for the first of May. I hated the thought of it, and I couldn't sleep for nights. I've always hated parties, the ones for me especially.

First thing in the morning, May first, 1934, I went to see the hyena.

"It's a pain," I told her, "but I've got to go to my party tonight."

"Lucky you," she answered. "I wish I could go too. I don't know how to dance, but I'm a good conversationalist."

"There'll be lots and lots to eat," I said. "I know, because I saw the caterers' trucks coming. They were all crammed full."

"And you're complaining?" she replied with a note of disdain. "I eat once a day, and you should see the crap they feed me!"

Just then I got a wild idea.

"Then why don't you go instead of me?" I chuckled.

"We don't look enough like each other," she answered, a little wistfully. "Believe me, if we did, I would!"

"Listen," I said. "At night the lights are down low, and no one sees that well anyhow. With a little disguise you'll pass in the crowd. Besides, we're just about the same size. And you're my only friend. Please... For me..."

The thought of our friendship must have given her pause. I saw she was thinking, and I knew she wanted to say yes. All of a sudden, she said:

"All right, I'll go."

It was terribly early, and there weren't many guards around. So I opened the cage and, in no time, the two of us were out in the street. I hailed a cab.

Back home they were all still in bed, fast asleep. We went to my room and I gave the hyena the dress I was supposed to wear that night. It was just a tiny bit long. She had a little trouble with my high heels too. Then there were her paws. They were really too hairy to pass for my hands. So I got her some gloves. Anyway, by the time the sun shone in, she could stand pretty straight, and she walked around my room a few times, just fine. We were both so busy that, when my mother came in to say "Good morning," the hyena just barely had time to hide under the bed.

"What on earth is that vile smell?" mother asked, as she opened the window. "You'd better take a bath before the party tonight!... And use my new bath salts."

"Of course, mamma," I answered.

She didn't stay long. The smell was too much for her.

"And don't be late for breakfast," she said as she left the room.

Now, what gave us the most trouble was finding some way to disguise the hyena's face. We thought for hours and hours. She turned down every one of my suggestions. Finally she said:

"I think I've got it. Do you people have a maid?"

"Yes," I told her, not sure what she was getting at.

"Fine! Then here's what we do. You ring for the maid, and when she comes in, we grab her and rip off her face. I'll wear it to the party over my own."

"There's only one hitch," I said. "I'm afraid it might kill her. Then someone is sure to find the body, and we'll both wind up in prison."

"Don't worry," the hyena answered. "I'm hungry enough to eat her."

"But what about the bones?"

"I'll eat them too. All right?"

"Well, only if you promise me you'll kill her first. Before you rip off her face, I mean. If not, it might hurt."

"No problem... No problem..."

I rang for Marie, the maid, still feeling a little uneasy about it all. I really wouldn't have done it if I didn't hate parties. When she came in I turned my head so I wouldn't have to look. I have to admit, it didn't take very long. A little scream and it was over. While the hyena ate her, I looked out the window.

After a few minutes, she told me:

"That's it. I can't eat another mouthful. I'm full. I managed to get through everything but the feet. Maybe you could let me put them in a bag. I could take them home and eat them later."

I pointed to the closet, still looking out the window.

"In there... There's a handbag... With little *fleurs-de-lys*... There are some handkerchiefs in it, but you can empty it out and use it."

She did. Then she said:

"Now turn around and see how pretty I look!"

She was standing, primping, in front of the mirror, wearing Marie's face. She had taken care to eat it very trim around the edges, to make sure it would fit.

"Yes, it's certainly nice and neat," I told her.

Toward evening, when the hyena was all dressed for the party, she confidently announced:

"I feel great! I've got a hunch I'm going to make a big hit!"

After the music downstairs had started, we waited a little while, then I said to her:

"All right, I guess it's time. Go on down. Just remember, be careful you don't sit next to my mother. She'll know it's not me. But she's the only one. None of the others know me."

I gave her a good luck hug and kiss as she left. She really smelled awful.

Outside it was already dark, and I was tired. The day had been hard on my nerves. To relax, I picked up a book and sat down by the open window. I remember, it was *Gulliver's Travels*, by Jonathan Swift. I hadn't been reading for an hour when I had an omen, a sign of things to come. A bat came flying in the window, with its shrill lit-

tle peeps. I've always been absolutely frightened to death of bats. My teeth began to chatter and I hid behind a chair. I was no sooner down on my knees, when a loud noise drowned out the fluttering of the wings. Someone was banging on the door. It was my mother. She came in, utterly livid with rage.

"Oh!" she shouted. "I never... Just now... Downstairs... We'd all just sat down when that... that thing that was sitting where you were supposed to be jumped up and yelled: 'So, I smell bad, do I? Well, you can keep your damn cake!' And all of a sudden it ripped off its face and began to chew it up. One leap, and, just like that, it was out the window..."

Leonora Carrington, *La Débutante*

Knit-Wit

or

The Thread of the Story

Never had I seen Lisa without her knitting needles. Which, in fact, she manipulated with an utterly stunning skill. It was her single passion, her sole occupation.

How disquieting, the sight of that superbly, indecently sensual flesh forever engaged in such a woefully banal pursuit.

It took me several months to coax her to put down her needles and her knitting, if only for a moment.

I lured her toward the bed. I was just about—at long last—to undress her, when I noticed, buried between two of her blond locks, a bit of woolen thread. I pulled it.

For two hours I pulled it. When I got to the end I had quite unraveled Lisa, and there, in her place, I was holding in my hands an immense ball of wool.

Jacques Sternberg, *Le Tricot*

IV

Of Death and Dying:
Ways & Means,
Whys & Wherefores

Of Tombs and Blooms

Ah, the lovely evenings! Before the glittering boulevard cafés, how many a woman in gaudy attire, how many an elegant ambler strutting and dawdling!

And the little flower-girls, walking to and fro with their baskets.

The lovely ladies, with nothing to do, accept flower gifts passed from hand to hand, blooms gathered up from who knows where?

"From who knows where?" you say?

Yes, quite! Because, dear ladies, there exists here in Paris a lugubrious trade, a business in league with a number of sumptuary funeral directors—and with gravediggers as well!—for the sole purpose of canvassing the morning's crop of corpses lest all those splendid bouquets, all those wreaths, all those roses that filial and conjugal piety heap on biers by the hundreds, day after day, be left to wither on their freshly dug graves and go utterly to waste.

Said flowers are almost always left behind once the somber rites are concluded. No one gives them another thought. Forgotten they lie in everyone's haste to leave. And rightly so...

It's then that our charming practitioners of eternal repose have themselves a fling. Far be it from the likes of them to overlook our flowers! Far be it from them to lose their heads in the clouds! Practical souls, these! Without a word they scoop them up by the armfuls. In the space of an instant they are heaving them over the cemetery wall and into a cart fortuitously placed for the occasion.

Two or three of the more scabrous and spry among them transport the precious cargo to the establishments of florist ladies of their acquaintance, who, with fairy-like fingers, deftly arrange those melancholic remains into corsage and nosegay of a thousand different styles, or even into bunches of solitary roses.

In time the little flower-girls of the evening appear, each with her basket. At the streetlamps' first light they walk up and down the boulevards, in front of the bright-lit terraces, and into the myriad establishments of pleasure.

And the blasé young beaus, eager to win over the elegant belles who have captured their fancy, purchase these flowers at prices beyond all reason and offer them to their ladies.

The latter, with faces powdered all white, accept them with a casual, indifferent little smile, holding them in their hands, or placing them perhaps in the cleft of their bosom.

And the glow from the gaslights turns their faces ghastly pale.

So it is that these spectral creatures, adorned with the flowers of Death, unwittingly sport the emblem of the love that they give and the love that they receive.

Auguste de Villiers de l'Isle-Adam, *Fleurs de ténèbres*

Of Waiter, Wine, and Water
or
A Buoyant Experience

That particular morning, it being a beautiful day, the tender, young, and lovely Clémentine had an idea.

Addressing her friend, a certain Monsieur Valgabourre, she suggested:

"Wouldn't it be nice to go out to the country?"

"The country?" retorted said individual sharply. "What the blazes is there to do out in the country?"

(Valgabourre's query was, in fact, somewhat more strongly phrased.)

"Nothing," replied the sensitive Clémentine. "Just go walking…"

"Where, for instance?"

"Anywhere you like… Bougival, perhaps…"

"Bougival?" snapped our vulgarian. "Would that make you happy?"

"Oh yes! Bougival!… That's where we met. Remember?"

"Ha! Better if I broke my leg that day instead!"

"You naughty thing," chided the gentle Clémentine. Then, persisting: "Well then, shall we go to Bougival?"

"Not bloody likely, woman!   We'll go in the other direction. To Joinville."

"If you like," she concurred.   "So, Joinville it is!"

"And I'm going to invite Arsaule to come with us."

"But..." she meekly objected.   "What do we need him tagging along for?"

"Damn!" Valgabourre sneered.   "Any more romantic strolls alone with you..."   And, with a gesture: "Up to here!...   But with Arsaule...   Well, at least he's good for a laugh."

"If you like, dearest...   Yes, let's invite Arsaule."

The individual in question, Valgabourre's closest friend, was one of that ill-bred and scoundrelly lot, always with his hand out, but, by common recognition, awfully good for a laugh.

As for their outing, it began much as expected.

In the train to Joinville, Valgabourre and Arsaule had a rollicking time offending a number of unaccompanied ladies and several young children.

So much so that, once arrived, they had worked up an appetite of rather considerable proportions.

The sweet-tempered Clémentine was quite hungry too.

At length, as the trio sat *al fresco* in a beergarden-cum-café along the Marne's flowered banks, the churlish Valgabourre, impatient, began to bellow:

"Ho!   Somebody!...   Where in hell are you, you damnable barkeep?   Isn't anyone going to serve us?"

.

With the witty Arsaule adding:

"Yea, verily, we are the most ill-served swains in all the realm!"

Clémentine, meanwhile, was lovingly caressing a large black cat, purring. (The cat, that is.)

At last, an elderly waiter in the establishment's employ doddered over to their table.

"What will madame and messieurs be having, please?" he quavered.

"What kind of swill is there to eat in this filthy hole?" Valgabourre elegantly queried.

"Beefsteak, chops, cutlets…"

Et cetera, et cetera… No need to go into the dismal details.

Now, it happened that, as the waiter was attempting to open their wine, the cork—owing either to its inferior quality or to the hireling's ineptitude—broke up and went crumbling into a thousand little pieces.

Well, you can picture the scene, I'm sure!

"Damn son of a…!" shrieked Valgabourre.

"Damn son of a…!" echoed Arsaule, even louder.

(I leave to your imagination the precise wording of their rather banal invectives, appropriately tailored to the occasion.)

The poor old waiter was mortified.

"It's... Please, its... It's nothing," he stammered. "Here, just let me..."

And he stood there, trying, with the end of a teaspoon, to fish out the crumbs of cork floating in the bottle of *vin* very *ordinaire*.

"Are you out of your bloody mind?" Valgabourre protested.

And Arsaule, in terms more unutterably vulgar still, demanded another bottle.

"And be quick about it!" he growled.

It was then that the poor old waiter appealed to their compassion.

The owner was already none too pleased with his work. If he lost a whole bottle of wine because of him... If they made him take back that bottle... Well, no question, he would have his excuse to throw him out on his ear... God knows, the job wasn't all that wonderful. It was just that, being here in Joinville, don't you know... Close to his daughter... Especially now, with her new baby and all...

"Take that for your brat!" barked the oh-so-clever Arsaule, with an obscene gesture that I surely needn't specify. "Another bottle!" I said. "And on the double, damn it!"

At which point the tender-hearted Clémentine interjected:

"Please, my good man, leave that bottle here. I'll drink it myself."

"But..."

"I love cork," she assured him in her angelic soprano. "Really, I simply adore it!"

And the dear child was true to her word.

As the jackassinine duo looked on, all a-twitter and a-chaff, she proceeded to quaff down the entire bottle, cork and all, to the last drop, dreg, and crumb.

Smiling her cherubic smile all the while.

★

Which is doubtless why, later that afternoon, when their canoe capsized and the two men drowned, Clémentine, buoyed up by all the cork she had ingested, was the only one to stay afloat.

I should mention that she married her rescuer, a fine young man recently graduated from the Ecole Polytechnique, and of excellent family.

Alphonse Allais, *Bonté récompensée*

From Collection to Collation
or
A Consuming Passion Consumed

Perhaps you will recall the disturbing case of that collector of macabre paraphernalia, and trappings from the world of crime, whose prized possession—the detachable collar of a celebrated guillotine victim—was laundered, starched, and ironed by an overly zealous housekeeper quite unimpressed by historical artifact.

A similar case occurred a number of years ago—more than a number—in the life of an old aristocrat of my acquaintance, the marquis de Bocherie.

Quite the roué and rake in his day, this marquis!

A rich, handsome chap, sturdily put together, de Bocherie—a skirt-chasing lecher untiring in his pursuits, with no fear of God and on close terms with the Devil—was the scourge of every husband in the regions.

I say "regions," plural, advisedly. Because, as well as being a fickle and frivolous profligate, the marquis, in his youth, was a landowner of consequence, and used to change his whereabouts as easily as his shirts.

But alas! one cannot possess one's cake and consume it as well, to coin a phrase worthy of our journalistic establishment.

With the passing of the years the marquis de Bocherie had grown old. Likewise his former ladyfriends.

What's more, buffeted from pillar of mortgage to post of insolvency, His Marquisship's domains (plural) had, in time, been broken up, divided, and scattered to the winds of ignominious public auction.

He had frittered away his francs with such clangorous and boisterous abandon that, at length, in the cruel franc-less silence that ensued, without two left to clink together, not even the most perceptive of eyes could detect their merest trace. Except, that is, in the purses of others.

Of his many ancestral lands only one had been left intact. And even too much intact. For it had been a good twenty years since any gardener had put a spade to its soil; or any woodsman, an axe to the lofty growth of its patrician chestnuts.

And yet, alone and wearied of the world, our blasé marquis had, one fine day, discovered amidst the shriveled fibers of his old parchment heart, a fiber fresh and green, alive and a-quiver, like the strings of a whole blessèd factory of harps all vibrating together.

De Bocherie, in fact, was now consumed by an obsession, a passion: the folly, the mania, the delirium of the collector.

And of what, good grief!

The marquis was collecting beans. (Podded, to be sure.)

Now, you who have spent time in the country know your beans, no doubt. As for the rest of you, *tant pis*, you'll have to take my word.

So, just imagine between four and five thousand beans (forty-five hundred, to be precise), of which even the most seemingly similar, identical in fact, proclaimed—nay, veritably screamed out—a world of difference to the connoisseur's discerning eye.

There were white beans, black beans, blue, and red, and violet beans. Beans with stripes, mottled and speckled beans. Beans of several hues at once: yellow and purple, orange and blue, red and green…

In short, not merely beans, but an utterly, absolutely polychromatic symphony!

De Bocherie, who knew his collection by heart, down to the last specimen, and who loved the beans as if they were his children, kept them all in a huge salad bowl, almost brimming over.

And every morning the marquis would contemplate the objects of his all-consuming passion, and tell himself, with the grandiloquence of a bygone era: "Methinks I must sort them! Methinks I must sort them!"

But every day, as dusk would descend upon the plain, the precious collection had not yet been sorted.

One sparkling spring morning de Bocherie had just gone out with his old dog and his old rifle to shoot some young rabbits.

Moments later, the manor's rusty little bell cawed out a few vague sounds, none too pleasant at best, but rendered all the more hostile by the brusque grating rasp of the corroded metal rod that set it swinging.

What passed for a servant—an ugly old crone, extraordinarily unkempt—came and opened the door. Her linguistic sophistication and ingenuity left much to be desired.

"So?" she queried.

"We've come to see the marquis de Bocherie. Is he at home?"
"Out!" she croaked.

"Ah? Will he be returning soon?"

"Humph!" she replied, with a noncommittal shrug.

Following which somewhat debatable reception, the two visitors took it upon themselves to enter.

"I am the nephew of the marquis de Bocherie," said the gentleman, "and this is my wife. We shall wait here for my uncle."

Their long walk in the fresh air had clearly given our visitors an appetite, for the young woman exclaimed:

"What say we make lunch while we're waiting?"

Consulted on the matter, the old crone, eyes raised heavenward, shrugged again and muttered another "humph!"

Losing patience, the marquis's niece insisted, in her most imperious of tones:

"Go slaughter us a duck and fetch me some eggs! And be quick about it, hear?"

Then, poking about the manor, she happened upon the famous salad bowl replete with its beans.

There took place, at that moment, an event most assuredly unprecedented in the annals of collection history.

The young woman proceeded to cook up the collection. When the collection was cooked, the young woman drained and strained it with great care.

Then the young woman put the collection into a skillet with butter and onion, the latter cut up into thin round slices.

In no time the venerable de Bocherie manor was smelling delicious.

Flames were lapping their flashing tongues against the skillet, as it sang out a hymn to life, to love, to glory.

Just, in fact, as the old marquis was coming through the door…

Now, I leave to your imagination all the cries of "uncle dear" that welcomed his arrival.

☆

The table was set.

First, a fine bacon omelette, then a fine duck, and then...

And then...

And then... the beans!

The marquis knew at once.

He recognized his white beans, his blacks, his blues, his reds, his violets. He recognized his yellow and purple beans, his orange and blues, his red and greens...

De Bocherie lurched erect, flailed the air with his long wizened arms, and fell backward, collapsing against an ancient Louis the Thirteenth clock, mute no doubt since Louis the Twelfth at least.

He was dead.

☆

The moral?

Make fun of collectors as much as you like. Only never, never make them eat their collection. Not even sautéed with onions...

Alphonse Allais, *La Fin d'une collection*

Money Is Time
or
The Poor Beggar and the Good Fairy

Once upon a time there was a certain Poor Beggar. The poorest of the poor as miserable Poor Beggars go...

Merciless and without reprieve, his ill star had shone relentlessly upon him. An ill star of most anemic, sickly hue... Of ill stars by far the illest—save one or two perhaps—in a century fraught with ill stars aplenty...

That morning he had gathered together the few sorry coins from the pockets of his waistcoat.

The sum thus assembled composed a total capital of one and ninety. (One franc and ninety centimes, that is...)

Enough for that day... But the next? Poor Beggar!...

And, smudging a few drops of ink on his frock coat's threadbare seams, he left, hoping against illusory hope that, at last, that day he might indeed *find work*.

The garment in question, long since a proper black, had, by and by, been faded by Time, that master dyer, into a coat of green. Our Poor Beggar would even refer to it now as such: "My green coat..." he would say, without batting an eye.

As for his old silk hat, of erstwhile black as well, it had, with age, turned distinctly reddish. (Ah, Nature's capricious contradictions!)

Coat and hat, in fact, went rather well together.

Each setting off the other, the green seemed all the greener, and the red all the redder... So much so that, for many a passerby, the Poor Beggar was nothing but some color-mad eccentric.

His day, alas, was one endless, frantic hunt... Staircases trudged up and down a thousand times... Calling here, calling there... Vestibules haunted for hours and hours on end... And with nothing, as usual, to show for all his pains...

Poor Beggar!

To save time and money, that day he hadn't eaten.

(Spare your pity: that day was no different from all the rest.)

Toward six o'clock that evening, exhausted, the Poor Beggar let himself collapse at the table of a little boulevard bistro on the edge of the city.

A nice little pub, and one he knew well, where, for four paltry sous they would sell you an absinth unequaled round about...

Ah! "A swallow of paradise," as some writer or other once put it. Four sous' worth in a glass... A taste of ecstasy for any Poor Beggar!...

Well, no sooner had ours wet his lips on the liquid rapture than a stranger came in and took a seat at the next table.

The newcomer, a being of more than human beauty, watched with an infinite and kindly compassion as the Poor Beggar sat trying to benumb his distress with sparing little sips.

"You look rather less than happy, Poor Beggar," observed the stranger, in dulcet tones that called to mind a choir of angels.

"Less? Ha!… Quite a bit less, my friend…"

"Tsk tsk!… Poor Beggar, I find you very pleasing and would like to do whatever I can to bring you joy… I happen to be a Good Fairy, you see… So! Tell me… What would it take to make you perfectly happy?"

"Me? Happy?" replied the Poor Beggar. "I'm sure I could make do nicely with a hundred sous a day… Every day for the rest of my life, I mean…

"A hundred sous? That's all?" the Good Fairy queried. "Five francs a day?… I must say, you're certainly not too demanding, Poor Beggar!… That being the case, your wish is hereby granted!"

Five francs a day for the rest of his life! The Poor Beggar was beaming.

The Good Fairy continued:

"Only, since I do have better things to do than come here and bring you your five francs every morning, and since I can easily know how long you're going to live… Well, if you have no objection I'll simply give it to you all, here and now. In one lump sum…"

In one lump sum!

Just imagine the look on the Poor Beggar's face!

In one lump sum!

Not only was he promised five francs a day... A whole hundred sous... But, what's more, he was about to receive it all now, in one lump sum!

The Good Fairy, having completed the necessary calculations, and exclaiming "Here's the total, Poor Beggar," threw down on his table the lump sum of seven francs, fifty centimes.

Seven and a half francs, that is. (Or a hundred fifty sous, for the uninitiated...)

The Poor Beggar, in turn, calculated the length of time said lump sum represented.

One day and a half!

No more than a day and a half to live, Poor Beggar!

"Bah! Things have been worse," he muttered.

And, blithely taking himself in hand, he went off to feast on his seven francs fifty with certain dancing-girls of his acquaintance.

Alphonse Allais, *Le Pauvre Bougre et le bon génie*[1]

[1] My translation of Allais's dramatization of this text, entitled *The Poor Beggar and the Fairy Godmother*, appears in my collectiuon *A Flea in Her Rear, or Ants in Her Pants, and Other Vintage French Farces* (New York: Applause Theatre Books, 1994).

The Fatal Inflection

I knew a little old lady once, who looked like a fish. She had the profile of a carp, parted her hair down the middle, and wore a pair of ugly green glasses.

She lived off in a none-too-fashionable quarter, in perpetual fear and trembling, and in a tiny apartment that she didn't want to leave. For sentimental reasons. Her parrot had died there. No ordinary bird... It could swear in five languages. Not that the little old lady would admit it...

Anyway, life in the tiny apartment had become unbearable. Next door was an artist's studio. And her neighbors, in fact, were painters. Now, it's common knowledge that, when a little old lady who looks like a fish and wears ugly green glasses has painters for neighbors, she's got to expect her share of practical jokes. And not always in the best of taste, I might add...

Whether she expected them or not, I can't say. But she had her share, believe me. Like the day she went to answer the doorbell and found herself face to face with a skeleton. The one they used for anatomy... Draped in a Spanish cape, hands on hips, with a lighted cigarette dangling from its teeth, and smiling its eternal smile... Or the day she found a milkpail hanging from her doorknob, filled to the brim with various and nefarious liquids, mixed up in one unspeakable concoction...

I won't bother to go into the more commonplace pranks. Like letters announcing great winnings in the lottery, or sudden huge inheritances...

Well, all things considered, you can imagine her relief when

she found out, one day, that her painters were moving. It seems they hadn't been bothering to pay their rent. Eight or nine months' worth...

And so, the little old lady jumped—literally—for joy, and clicked her heels, and danced a little jig around her tiny apartment. Then, puffing and panting, she sat down in her chair to have herself a laugh. But suddenly an awful thought flashed through her addled brain. That damnable studio... No doubt it would be rented to another herd of painters, and life, once more, would become unlivable...

From that moment on it was more fear and trembling. For weeks and weeks... Until, one day, she noticed that the studio had been rented.

You can picture how she stood, eyes peeled and door ajar, peering at everything the movers brought in... But where were the paintings? The canvasses? The easels?... Could it be that the new tenant wasn't a painter after all?... The thought was almost too exquisite to bear. Again the little old lady jumped for joy, and clicked her heels, and danced a little jig. This time she broke her ugly green glasses, but what did it matter?... Then, as she sat down, wheezing and coughing, to have herself another laugh, a second thought occurred to her, in a flash of despair. If he wasn't a painter, then maybe he was a sculptor. And wasn't that just as bad? Who knows? Maybe worse!... So the little old lady, in her accustomed fear and trembling, decided to find out once and for all by asking the concierge.

When she made her way downstairs, there, standing by the door, was the new neighbor himself! A massive young man, built like a locomotive and swarthy as a fine Havana cigar... He was talking with the concierge in a thunderous voice that made the glass pane tremble. But what struck her most of all were his piercing, wild-eyed stare, his shaggy lion's mane—all tangles and snarls, like the plot of a bad play—and a jutting lower jaw that looked ready to take a bite. The head of a mad assassin, if ever she saw one...

The little old lady jumped back in alarm, too frightened to approach, and beat a retreat, pattering up the stairs like a mouse when it hears someone say the word "cat."

Next morning, after nightmares filled with rapine and murder, she went scurrying downstairs to ask the concierge precisely what this fearsome new neighbor was. But the concierge, as luck would have it, was deaf as a post, and all the little old lady could get out of her was the fact that he was an artist.

Now, for her the word "artist" could mean only one thing. Well, two... Painter or sculptor... The fact is, the young man was actually an actor. A tragedian, to be exact... And he needed all the space in a studio to rehearse in. To emote and thrash about with plenty of room to spare. It seems he was unable to mention the fires of hell without pacing at least ten yards in every direction. Add the brimstone, and he would soon be out the door, gesticulating in the street.

In order to set the proper mood for his roles, the young man had done over the studio in black. Black hangings on the walls, sprinkled with silver sequins, with a skull and crossbones perched in each corner... Black ceiling, studded with pale stars here and there... An enormous black bed, like a bier, where he slept... And on both sides of the bed, at night, two gigantic candles, flickering their eerie glow over this rather singular—and none-too-jovial—retreat...

For the first few days, despite her apprehension, the little old lady had no real cause for concern. But soon she began to give a shudder, now and then, at certain loud noises... Great thumping sounds that made the whole house shake... She had no idea, of course, that it was merely the actor pounding out the rhythm of his lines with his foot... And then it happened. One evening she opened her door to go get dinner. At about six o'clock... Suddenly she was taken aback as a cavernous voice bellowed out: "Prepare to die!"

The little old lady stood agape on the landing, listening transfixed. Even stronger, the voice boomed again: "Prepare to die!"

She clutched at the banister, growing weak and faint with

fright. "Yes, yes! Prepare to die!" thundered the voice once more.

This time it was clear that the gruesome warning was coming from behind the new neighbor's door. What she failed to realize, of course, was that the actor, quite simply, was rehearsing his lines, and trying to find just the right inflection.

And so, not doubting for a moment that a crime was being committed, the little old lady began trembling from head to toe, like a bowlful of jelly. She wanted to run... To go call the police... But her legs wouldn't move. They just buckled beneath her. And all she could do was sit in a heap on the top step of the staircase, and try to catch her breath.

At that moment the studio door flew open and the tragedian appeared. The little old lady cast a quick glance inside, through her broken green glasses... Much to her surprise, she noticed no cadaver. But the black-draped walls and the skulls and crossbones sent chills up her spine. Her neighbor, she was certain now, was some latter-day Bluebeard. There was no doubt about it... Summoning all her strength, she dragged herself down the stairs in an effort to warn the concierge of her discovery. But before she had a chance, there, behind her, once again, was that menacing admonition, that "Prepare to die!", whistling about her through the actor's clenched teeth, as he continued searching for just the right inflection.

Petrified with fear, she fled into the street. The actor, right behind, quite oblivious to it all, kept muttering under his breath: "Prepare to die!... Prepare to die!..."

"My God!" gasped the little old lady. "It's me... It's me he's after!" And she hailed a passing omnibus in utter desperation. It stopped. She clambered on... Inside there were two empty seats. The last two... The little old lady sat down in one, and heaved a great sigh... Until she noticed that, across, in the other, was her neighbor, who had just sat down too... Face contorted in a grimace, his eyes flashing wildly... Wringing and squeezing the handle of his umbrella, as if choking it to death, he kept moving his lips in that fateful, awesome phrase that she alone could hear: "Prepare to die!... Prepare to die!... Prepare..."

The omnibus rattled its way along. The actor mumbled. And the little old lady sat trembling in her boots...

Absorbed in his quest for dramatic perfection, our tragedian stared blankly through his unintended victim, who passed quickly from fear to horror, and from horror to sheer, unmitigated panic. She could hear his repeated, bloodthirsty threat in the rumble of the wheels and the rattle of the windows. She could see him, before her eyes, turning into a demon. Growing bigger... Bigger... Horns sprouting from his forehead, and eyes darting fire... She tried to get up... To run... To escape... But again her legs refused to move. And when she opened her mouth to scream, not a sound would pass her lips. Nothing but a terrified gasp...

Her last...

The little old lady with the profile of a carp dropped her head to one side. Her broken green glasses went slipping down her nose. And she sat there, without moving, looking very much asleep...

At the end of the line, the tragedian, still trying to find just the right inflection, went to have himself an absinth, never once suspecting that he had just carried off the most impressive triumph any actor could ever hope for...

Léon Xanrof, *La Vieille Dame et le tragédien*

Rogue Rug
or
Mourning Prayer

In the bedchamber sorrow and despair hung heavy. The poor woman was laid out, pale and lifeless, hands together on her bosom. Her eyelids had just been closed in death. Kneeling at the foot of the bed, her sister, palms joined in supplication, was praying:

"Dear God, I always loved you and served you, and never asked you for the least little favor in return… But my sister… My sister, whom I love with all my heart, is all I have in the world… Please God, I beg you, let there be a miracle! Let life return to this room that death has ravaged!"

Then it seemed she could hear the voice of the Almighty, saying:

"My child, thou wouldst have me set a most dangerous precedent. Long ago I decided, once and for all, that death was to be a final and irreversible event. If not, my regime would have constantly been faced with untold complications. Still, thou art a maiden of exceptional piety. And I am a romantic… So, wrong as thou art to ask me to violate my principles… Enough said… Let thy prayer be granted!"

No sooner had He pronounced these words than the corpse's eyelids fluttered… Her bosom heaved… Her lips parted… Life had, indeed, returned to that room that death had ravaged!

Life had returned…

The dead flies, stuck to the mirror, stretched out their little insect feet, flickered their myriad-faceted eyes, and flew joyously up to the ceiling…

Life had returned...

A little stuffed bird, perched on a hat in a shrubbery of ribbons and bows and paper flowers, flapped its wings, gave a joyful peep, then it too took flight, lit atop an armoire, and chirped out a song of triumph...

Yes, life had returned...

The lionskin rug by the bed raised its head and, opening its huge jaws wide, ate up everyone in sight.

Tristan Bernard, *Le Lion*

Saint Adorata
or
The Back Door to Heaven

One day I went to visit the little church at Szepeny, in Hungary, and was shown there a most holy and venerated relic.

"It contains," the guide told me, "the blessèd body of Saint Adorata. Some sixty years ago her grave was discovered not far from where we stand. Doubtless she had suffered martyrdom in the very first days of Christianity, during the Roman occupation, when the region about Szepeny was evangelized by Marcellinus, deacon of the early church, the same one who witnessed Nero's crucifixion of Saint Peter. It is supposed," he continued, "that Saint Adorata was converted by his preachings and that, after her martyrdom, her body was interred by Roman priests. Scholars assume that 'Adorata' was simply the Latin translation of her pagan name, whatever it might have been, since they doubt she was ever baptized, except by her own blessèd blood. Such a name, to be sure, is not one to inspire proper Christian thoughts. Still, the fact that her body was so perfectly preserved, and that it was found intact after being buried in the ground for so many centuries, was proof that, nonetheless, she was one of the Lord's elect, chosen to join the virgin choir in Paradise and sing His divine and everlasting glory… Ten years ago Saint Adorata was canonized in Rome…"

I only half-listened to his many speculations. Saint Adorata, after all, was hardly one of my especial concerns, and I was about to leave when, suddenly, I was struck by the sound of a long, deep sigh, moaning itself out beside me. It had come from a little old man, nattily dressed, and leaning on a coral-knobbed cane as he gazed intently at the shrine.

I left the church and the little old man came following out behind me. I turned around and noticed, once again, his elegant figure from an age long past. He smiled at me. I nodded back.

"Really, monsieur," he finally asked me, rolling his r's in French like a typical Hungarian. "Do you really believe all those theories the sacristan was babbling?"

"Heavens," I replied, "I have no opinion on such devotional matters!"

"You are only a visitor among us," he went on. "But I have wanted for so long now to tell someone the true story that I shall tell it to you, monsieur, on condition that you promise never to breathe a word of it to anyone hereabouts."

My curiosity had been piqued. I promised him what he asked.

"Well, monsieur," said the old man, "Saint Adorata was my mistress."

I gave a little start and pulled away, certain that I had a lunatic before me. Smiling at my surprise, he assured me with a tremulous quiver in his voice:

"No, monsieur, I am not mad. What I tell you is the truth. Saint Adorata was my mistress. And, had she consented, I would have made her my wife.

"I was nineteen years old when I met her. Today I am past eighty, and never, monsieur, never have I loved any other...

"My father was a wealthy landowner from the outskirts of Szepeny. Myself, I was a medical student. I had worked so hard and become so exhausted that the doctors insisted I rest. They said that a little travel would be a healthy change.

"And so I left for Italy. It was in Pisa, monsieur, that I met her, and at once she became the one and only thing I lived for.

Together we traveled to Rome, to Naples... Wherever we went our love made everything more beautiful... Finally we arrived in Genoa. I was going to bring her home with me... Here, to Hungary... To present her to my parents, to ask her to marry me, monsieur... Then one morning, I found her, beside me, lying dead..."

The old man paused in his tale for a moment. When he took it up again his voice, quivering and quavering even more than before, was barely above a whisper.

"I was able to prevent the innkeepers from learning of my lover's death, but only by ruse and artifice more worthy of a killer! When I think of it, monsieur, it still makes me shudder... No one, to be sure, suspected the slightest crime. They merely assumed that my companion had left that morning at a very early hour.

"I shall not trouble you by describing the horror of the long, long moments I spent with the corpse. How, versed as I was in anatomy, I expertly embalmed it... How I packed it in a trunk... All without arousing the slightest suspicion. The hustle and bustle of a good-sized inn with its many and sundry guests, coming and going when and where they pleased... The anonymity of it all was most helpful under the circumstances.

"Then came the trip home, and the customs inspection at the border. Thank God, I passed through it without incident. A miraculous tale... Miraculous, monsieur!... Still, by the time I reached Hungary I was sickly, pale, and wan. A shadow of myself...

"Among my effects I had brought back an ancient stone sarcophagus that I had purchased from an antique dealer while passing through Vienna. It was part of some famous collection, though I fear I have long since forgotten which one... Since my family always left me to my own devices and paid little attention to whatever I was about, they were not at all surprised at how much baggage I had brought with me, or how heavy it seemed to be...

"I myself engraved the inscription 'Adorata' and a cross on the sarcophagus, and in it I placed the body of my beloved, bound up with strips of cloth…

"Then one night, monsieur, with an effort beyond belief, I carried it into a nearby field and buried it in a spot known only to me, and that none but myself would be able to find. And every day, alone, I would come to that tomb to pray…

"One year went by… Then, one day, I was obliged to leave for Budapest. Imagine my despair when, two years later, upon my return, I found that a factory had been built on the very site where I had buried the treasure more precious to me than life itself!

"I nearly took leave of my senses, monsieur. I would have killed myself then and there were it not for the fact that our parish priest, visiting us that evening, told me how, while the field was being excavated for the foundations of the factory, the workers had dug up the sarcophagus of a Christian martyr from the Roman era, a woman, Adorata by name, and that they had removed the precious relic to our little village church.

"At first I was about to disabuse the good father and tell him of his error. But I quickly thought better of it, realizing that in the church I could gaze upon my beloved any time I might have a mind to do so.

"Besides, monsieur, my heart kept telling me that she was really not unworthy of the devotion bestowed upon her. To this day I feel that she deserves it, not only for her great beauty and matchless grace, but for that very passion that, perhaps, was what had killed her. What's more, she was good, and sweet-tempered. Whatever she and I had done, she was pious and devout. If only she had not died, monsieur, I would have made her my wife.

"And so I let events proceed as they would, and my love turned to worship. The object of my passion was declared worthy of veneration. A little later she was beatified, and fifty years after the discovery of her body, she was canonized. I went to Rome myself to attend the ceremony. It was the most magnificent spectacle I had ever witnessed in all my days.

"With it, monsieur, my beloved took her place in heaven. And me? I was happy as one of God's angels. I came back here quickly as I could, filled with the strangest and most sublime joy one could imagine, to worship at the shrine of Saint Adorata..."

With tears in his eyes, the little old man, nattily dressed, tottered off, tapping the ground with his coral-knobbed cane, and repeating over and over: "Saint Adorata... Saint Adorata..."

Guillaume Apollinaire, *Sainte Adorata*

Requiesc-Hat
or
A Grave Mistake

I thought I'd talk to you about my sister... It's kind of embarrassing, because whatever she does it always turns out awful for her! Still...

The only thing we ever do for fun, me and her, is go to funerals. Me, I'm crazy about them. Anybody's... So any time someone in the family croaks, off we go, the two of us! It's the only time both of us can ever get together...

Well, the other day we went to one for some old cousin of ours or other. Actually some cousin's grandmother... Kicked the bucket, like they say... "Pow!"... Just like that...

It was lovely, let me tell you. The church was crammed full of people, almost ready to burst... The church, that is... And beautiful? Pfff!... Flowers all over, everywhere you looked... Wreaths, bouquets... All kinds... Even carnations, if you can believe it... "Carnations?" I told them. "They're bad luck, didn't you know? She wouldn't like it..." (*With a shrug.*) Oh well...

It was lovely, like I said. With the bier in the middle, up high, and the coffin, all draped in black... A pretty shade... Very dark, like you'd expect... I mean, a light bier after all?... And the organ, playing a few nice jaunty tunes... To give a gay little touch, if you know what I mean... "Lovely"'s not the word... In fact, right then and there I couldn't help thinking: "Too bad she's not here, she'd really have a treat! It's like nothing they ever did for her when she was alive!..."

Well anyway, since we're Catholics my sister brought a hat.

Because for Catholics, in church, if you're a woman you've got to cover your head. With a hat or something... Anything, I suppose... That's just the way it is. It depends on the religion. A Moslem's got to leave his shoes at the door of the mosque... Jewish men, when they go to the synagogue, wear a hat and the women don't... Buddhists have to play with some kind of wooden noisemaker or other... Like I say, it depends... Everyone's got their special god and their special religion... The opium of the people, like they call it...

So my sister had her hat, like she was supposed to... One with flowers all over... Violets... A pretty little hat with lots and lots of violets... Little, like I say, but with all those violets it looked a lot bigger. Especially from the back... Anyway, there were these young people sitting behind us, who kept saying things like... I mean, you know how young people are, always joking... And they kept saying: "Oh là là! What a big hat!..." And "I'm missing the show!..." And "Damn! Did you ever see a hat with so many flowers?..." Things like that... So I said to my sister: "Never mind... Just take it off, that'll shut them up! I'm sure God'll forgive you..."

Well, she did. She took it off and laid it down in front of her... You know, where you kneel to pray... And things calmed down, and we sat listening to the service... It was lovely!... With the bier and all, and the coffin... But all of a sudden, then and there, there's the usher coming down the aisle. You know, the sexton... The sacristan... Whatever... Anyway, he looks in our pew and sees my sister's hat down there, and... Would you believe it? He thinks it's a wreath! With all those flowers, I mean... And he picks it up, brings it over, and puts it down on the bier with the rest of them.

Let me tell you, I was upset! Then the priest goes over with his incense and begins waving it all over my sister's hat. "Upset"'s not the word... But what upset me the most was afterwards, when we all had to line up and bless the body. I wish you could have seen us, one after another, sprinkling her hat with holy water!

She was depressed something awful, my sister... Awful... That afternoon I went to see her. Just in time too! A minute later and

I think she would have… Tsk tsk!… Really, that's how depressed… And crying?… "Boo hoo! Boo hoo!…" Crying her eyes out… I tell her: "Listen, she lived to a ripe old age! Why are you bawling?…" "'She?' Who?" she says. "I'm crying about my hat!"

So that night I went to the cemetery to see if maybe I could get it back. I wish you could have seen me! It was horrible!… Brrr!… "Horrible"'s not the word… I mean, I'm not crazy about cemeteries at night. Or in the daytime either, for that matter… Not exactly what I call fun… Funerals are one thing, but cemeteries… Well, there I am. It's cold, and the wind is blowing "Hoooh! Hoooh!" over the gravestones, and going like "Psssh! Psssh!" through the trees… No fun at all… And me, I'm stumbling and tripping… Two, three times… And sneezing and sneezing… Four times at least… And… Anyway, I finally find the grave, and the flowers… And my sister's blessèd hat…

Just one problem… The caretaker saw me coming… "Who the hell are you?" he asks me. "What the hell do you think you're doing?"

"I came to get my sister's hat," I tell him.

"Are you balmy? 'Sister's hat' my ass!" he tells me. "I know your kind! You're one of them bastards who come and steal the flowers off graves, then go out the next day and sell them for weddings! Damn graverobbers!"

Well, he carts me away to the station. And there I am, screaming that it's my sister's hat, damn it! They wanted to lock me up. Then my sister comes in. "I'm telling you, that's my hat!" she tells them.

So they locked the two of us up. Together… Twice in one day… Me? I was really going cuckoo… Believe me, "cuckoo"'s not the… "I'm telling you, it's my sister's hat! It's my sister's hat, I'm telling you!…"

Well, lucky for us the priest finally showed up and managed to get us out.

Just one thing... Do me a favor, you people. If you happen to come to my funeral, and if you don't want any trouble, please, no flowers!

Fernand Raynaud, *Ma sœur et son chapeau*

Behind Closed Doors
or
Of Tide and Time

They had met during the summer at a seaside resort and had spent their days boating, drunk with the sun, and their nights, making love, drunk with one another.

In fact, they shared the same passion for those two pursuits, sex and sailing, which they found more intoxicating, to be sure, than any others. Understandably, since they were both only twenty, and were half-heartedly taking courses that would, one day, oblige them to molder in drab bureaucratic occupations, than which they couldn't possibly find anything more loathsome.

Living, as they did, in a big city watered only by a river hardly more than a sewer, they found themselves, come autumn, deprived for long months of the pleasures of the random sail, and took out their yearnings on every magazine and book filled full with talk of halyards and riggings, rudder blades and bowsprits. They wouldn't miss a film even vaguely to do with the water, or especially those documentary marathons that touted the heady joys of waterski, surfboard, and such; and in January they spent ten whole hours every day at the annual yacht show.

From time to time, too, they would wander the usually deserted halls of their city's naval museum, though less often, and not overly enthralled. And yet it was there, one day, that they both got an utterly irrational urge, and one that took shape as an act they could scarcely have conceived of or planned out beforehand.

Repulsed by the fulsome, offensive pageantry of naval warfare in all its forms, their sole interest there was in the saga of sail: its dramas, its grand epics, its staggering challenges and nightmarish horrors. The latter above all, since those who were sailors themselves, used to challenging the sea, could relive them first-hand. Which is how it happened that, one winter day, our young couple was particularly taken by the sight of a large inflatable life raft sitting on the floor in a room devoted to the flotsam and assorted memorabilia of history's most legendary naval adventures. Like a huge tire, half covered with a moldy tarpaulin, it looked for all the world as if it had drifted over thousands of miles, braving all the swells and tides and terrors that the sea served up so freely, only to land just there where it sat, spat up by the breaking surf.

The selfsame idea came to both of them at once: to hide out in some dark corner until closing, then spend the night in that raft, like castaways, survivors of a sinking boat, set adrift on the water.

Hiding was no problem, and as soon as all the doors were closed they stole through the shadows and into the raft of their dreams and fancies. Shining a pocket flashlight, they found their nautical retreat supplied with everything one might need to survive the sea's caprice: sextant, compasses, maps, paddles, signal sail, blankets, medicine kit, gas stove, distress flares, deep-sea fishing gear... Everything, that is, except for food and drinking water. A museum didn't usually display perishables, after all. For a moment the young woman kicked herself for not thinking to bring a few sandwiches for an evening snack, but playing the game to the hilt would only give it that much more charm. Besides, in no time they were cuddling very close in their rubber niche, and their hunger for each other soon made them forget their forced abstinence from food.

They slept long and soundly. And not without realizing, when they woke, that, had they really been lying there, soaked through and through, bobbing at the mercy of the storm-tossed tide, the night would not have been quite so serene.

Several things began to disturb them, however, when they finally dragged themselves out of their shipwreck refuge. On the one hand it was ten o'clock already and they didn't hear a thing, not the least sign of life. What's more, they had let themselves get shut up in a large enclosed space without windows or skylight, and although it opened out onto one of the exhibit rooms, it was closed off from it by a sliding grill stretched across and planted firmly in the opposite wall, with bars as solid-looking as those of a prison cell. Worst of all, not only would our floor-flotsam heroes have given anything for a cup of hot coffee, but they were also beginning to get rather hungry. They scoured every inch of their thirty-by-thirty-foot space, crammed as it was with models and pictures, old rigging and grappling hooks, objects of all sorts made of wood or copper, cast-iron or bronze, but nowhere did they find a single water tap to drink from or the slightest crumb to feed on, not even a frozen fish, or a can of something, or a package of biscuits.

The whole day not a soul came into the building. Not a visitor, not a guard, not even the night watchman, They told themselves finally that it must be the one day a week when the place was closed. But the next day nothing changed: still nobody, no sign of life, not a footstep…

The day after that only one thought obsessed them: to escape from their cage and find the way out. But they struggled in vain for hours to dislodge the steel grill, which could only be opened electronically from outside. They looked high and low for a few drops of water, anything to nibble… But no, not a thing… At last hunger and thirst began gnawing away their strength, driving their minds to the edge of madness. And little by little, as the hours ticked doggedly by, their resistance gave way, in a frenzy of terror, to the deep chill of panic and the total collapse of logic.

The logic of the banal, of the everyday occurrence. Commonplace, at least, in the outside world, beyond the enclosure where our two continued to stagnate. Quite simply, since the evening when they had had themselves sealed up in the nautical mausoleum, the guards, after giving the usual ultimatums, had gone out on strike. The negotiations were dragging on longer than expected, no agreement could be reached.

The strike lasted, in fact, for twelve days, exactly.

Jacques Sternberg, *Survie*

Over and Over...
and Over

Returning home and about to go in, he was struck by the realization that he had been living for forty years in the same three-room flat on the fourth floor of the same building.

Never before had he given it a thought. Or rather, for all those forty years, he might have occasionally said to himself that he was glad or fed up, contented or upset, to be back in his place, but it would never have occurred to him to express that banal situation in actual figures.

Forty years... And since he only rarely stayed out all night, and went away even less, he was obliged to admit that he had gone into his flat some fourteen thousand times, and, in all likelihood, had left it fourteen thousand times as well. Which meant that he had had to climb up six hundred thirty thousand steps, since his building had no elevator, and to climb down six hundred thirty thousand too. In his flat he must have shaved a good ten thousand times and drunk more than twenty-five thousand cups of coffee, tons and tons of water, and all that just so he could go take more than thirty thousand leaks. Not to mention the fourteen thousand times he had woken up in the same bed, facing in the same direction for all of those forty years, stuck against the same wall, whose paper hadn't changed one bit either in all that time.

Nor could he take any comfort in tallying up his incidental pastimes and distractions.

Indeed, he had always lived by his pen and had never written a line outside his flat. Which obviously meant that, having published some fifty hack novels, he must have written at least twenty thousand pages, rough drafts included, and bits and pieces that had never got finished. On the other hand, he didn't consider himself a reading freak, and probably hadn't read more than five thousand books in all. But since he had always enjoyed jazz more than literature, he owned over four thousand LP's and had listened to each one at least three times, some more. Likewise, either out of weak will or habit, he had always watched at least one TV film a day, which meant that, again, he had passed the ten thousand mark.

All that left him considerably aghast.

Never before had he realized with such clarity—now that he had rounded the corner of sixty-five—how, since twenty-five, he had been repeatedly carrying out these automatic actions with more and more lassitude, and less and less conviction.

It was then that, during the evening, he quite understandably made up his mind to perform one action that he had never before performed in that flat. To wit, he filled up the bathtub with hot water and gently eased himself in, after slashing his wrists.

Jacques Sternberg, *Le Répétitif*

Quo Vadis?
or
The Marathon

He was running.

On a grayish earth spreading out on all sides over a barren land-scape, with nothing, not a tuft of grass, not even a few pebbles. And all around, a kind of vague light, like dusk dimmed through the mist.

He was running easily along, not the least bit tired. Which surprised him since he was never big on hiking or jogging for his health. Then too, about that health, there was that thought he could-n't get out of his head, that memory, fresh in his mind, of being sud-denly struck down, laid low with a raging fever, and seeing in one last flash some doctor he didn't know, called at dawn, still hearing him in his mind announcing that he'd better get himself right to the hospital, no doubt about it.

But now there he was, far from a hospital bed, and he was running. A marathon, probably, since he seemed to know that he'd been running for some time. A good, steady pace, no shortness of breath, not too fast, not too slow. And he didn't see anyone in front of him or in back, so he told himself that he must be way ahead or way behind in this race that seemed to go on and on, with no end.

That is, until that moment when he thought he could make out, looming up from the hazy shadows, two poles, and stretched between them an enormous, gaudy banner. He felt sure now that it must be a marathon, because there was the word "FINISH" spread out in black letters over the banner, unruffled by the slightest breath of wind.

Without slowing down, still without a hint of fatigue, he passed between the poles.

And in the space of a second he had the terrifying realization that he ought to have stopped, that now it was too late, too late forever and ever...

Jacques Sternberg, *Le Marathon*

Bottled Up
or
The Genie

A swarm of hornets is buzzing inside his skull.

Eyes closed, he crouches motionless, knees bent up to his chest, forehead flat against the hard, cold ground. The kitchen tiles, no doubt.

This time he went too far.

He feels himself full to the brim with an acrid, sickish liquid. He knows that to move the least little bit will send it spilling over.

From time to time the swarm moves off. Then it's those damnable churchbells clanging, with their dozen clappers pealing out his pulse.

Part his lips just a little and he'd puke himself inside out, completely. Leave nothing but a slimy carcass on the floor.

He can't remember how much he swilled down. An echo of champagne burns a path up his gullet. It was after the movie. They went to see a Billy Wilder film, one where Audrey Hepburn and Humphrey Bogart keep drinking champagne. Béatrice was laughing all the way home. So what was it that made her start yelling at him later? Because he suggested they pop open a bottle too?

Just thinking makes his head hurt. Thoughts, recollections, shaken and jarred like shrill little chimes…

No, she didn't yell right away. He suggested they should open the Dom Pérignon he was keeping on ice, and at first all she did was make a snide pun on the name. On "dumb" or "damn"... Or on "doom." He can't remember.

He popped it open anyway. Béatrice hates for him to drink, says he's becoming an alcoholic, even though she knows he isn't. She only wants to put him down, make him think that he's a has-been, that he can't write anymore.

He never drinks whiskey. Nothing but wine.

No gin, no vodka, that sort of thing, no tequila. None of those manufactured, artificial drinks. Oh, once in a while a little sip of scotch or a few drops of plum liqueur in his coffee. Even then...

Béatrice isn't anything at all like Audrey Hepburn. Audrey Hepburn never yells. She has the look of a fawn, a long graceful neck, lots of sparkling white teeth. She never finds fault when her men drink champagne.

Béatrice did take a glass after all. She didn't say a word, just drank it. Only one.

Again, those churchbells...

He decides to open one eye, thinks better of it. The slightest flash of light would kill him for sure. Begin by stretching his legs. Easily, gently, so as not to spill over.

What is this, where is he?

First his right leg, slowly.

He no sooner makes a move than a great gushing swell sends him reeling, rolling about like a marble. Again there he is in a weird position, left leg bent up under him, right one out straight, head turned with one cheek pressed against the tiles. Now to unbend the left, gradually, and stretch flat on his stomach... But suddenly the swirling tide lets loose. He clenches his teeth, jaws tight, not to puke.

His gut pulled in one direction, his skin in the other.

Finally he's straightened out both legs. Odd how, as he lies there, face down, the floor feels so smooth, convex, as if bulging, pregnant with a promise of ills to come.

What was it that happened next? Béatrice went into the kitchen, rinsed out her glass. He remembers the water running, how it sounded like a kind of reproach that wouldn't stop. He poured himself another champagne, his third. He's not one to be put off by a little temper tantrum.

He'd felt like having a party for himself, staying in a world where every woman would be an Audrey Hepburn, where every man could phone his secretary from the car and tell her to get him two tickets on the next ship out... "No matter where, Sonia..."

That's not Béatrice's kind of people. For her the ideal man is a cross between Lord Byron, say, and an economist. Someone who can quote the Dow Jones average and the latest Duras novel, who drinks Schweppes Light and signs petitions against the forced assimilation of the Samoyed ethnic minority of the Altaic plateau. That kind...

It was hardly a party. Béatrice came back from the kitchen with her somber stormy-weather look. As she zipped down her dress she said something or other that didn't register on his brain.

He decides to try opening his left eye. The lid moves, flutters. Is he really in the kitchen? At first all he sees is a thick greenish haze. Little by little he makes out vague forms, can't tell what they are. Nothing looks like anything, nothing that he knows. Like his own life, really. Yes, now he can admit it. Shapeless, chaotic.

He must have finished off the bottle by himself, slouched in a living room chair listening to Queen singing "We will, we will rock you..." Not at all his kind of music, but it's a writer's duty, he always says, to keep up with the times. To understand the taste of the younger generations even though he doesn't share it. The fact is, he can't stomach them any more than their music. The adolescents especially. He loathes them all, thinks they're ugly, arrogant, lazy. But he's not going to give up such a potential public and let his rivals in the trade take them over. The cleverer, or more popular, or younger ones than himself. So he's learned their language, hobnobs with them at their concerts, even at their bashes, writes articles for their teenage rags and girlie mags. Does his absolute damnedest…

Béatrice makes fun of him for dressing the way he does. Wearing tie-dyed shirts, torn jeans, baggy jackets, or sunglasses in the middle of winter. To her way of thinking a literary type should always be clean shaven, wear tweed jackets with open-collar shirts and silk ascot ties. She can't understand that, at forty-five, if he doesn't want to tune out for good and fall by the wayside he's got to keep up with the changing styles, the fads, the new trends in the air. "Hot air," Béatrice calls it.

No, it had to be more than just one bottle of champagne to pull him apart this way, body and mind. This time he did go too far, no doubt about it. He'd get up and check the fridge if not for those damnable hornets that are bound to come buzzing back. Check to see if those two bottles of Sauvignon Blanc he's been saving are still there, on the bottom shelf.

Suddenly he feels that his hand is all wet, in a puddle on the floor. He twists his head upright, leans it on his chin, tries to open both eyes together. Never mind the pounding of that energetic company of blacksmiths beneath his scalp… Yes, his right hand is half hidden in some kind of brownish liquid. Exactly what, it's impossible to tell in the green shadows that engulf him.

Again he shuts his eyes… Just what was it he did last night, after listening to Queen? He doesn't recall leaving, only seeing Béatrice come storming out of the bedroom, looking half asleep, her oversize T-shirt pulled down to her thighs. He remembers now how beautiful he thought she looked, how much he wanted to have her. Especially when she unplugged the stereo with a single silent tug. How sorry he felt, for one vague moment, that somehow he didn't seem to please her anymore, to amaze her, amuse her…

Unless his memory is playing tricks, he thinks he remembers pulling up her T-shirt and trying to pat her bottom.

He decides to try sitting on his haunches, cross his legs. Not an easy task. A frightening one even. No matter, he'll take his time, all he needs… He tries to maneuver himself into position, slips, collapses in the puddle. The strong smell of stale, tacky wine overwhelms him. With a lurch, in pain and rage, he gets up, wants to steady his body against the slick wall. It too slips from his grasp. Again he's sitting down… Feeling as though his eyes are being plucked from his head, or sucked out by leeches. He can't make out a thing. Nothing he can be sure of in that haunting green light. He's waiting now, waiting for the battering ram between his temples to stop its beating back and forth…

He must have drunk the Sauvignon after all. But certainly not both bottles. He's no drunkard, no matter what Béatrice is always saying. Or Jean-Paul either, who tells him he must have done his teething on a cork, and jokes that he hits the bottle so much it's a wonder he doesn't break his hand some day. Jean-Paul, his best friend. And Béatrice's best friend too.

Maybe he really did drink both bottles. And, a little later, even what was left of the Merlot from the day before. Half a liter or so… All of a sudden now, that image again: Béatrice, furious, his hand trying to lift her T-shirt and stroke her bottom. She turns, with a look on her face like none he's ever seen, that he couldn't describe, but that must have something to do with the slap in the face she gives him. A real "heavy metal" slap. Just the thought sets off that damn frenzy of bells again.

That's when she started yelling. He asked her to stop, kept telling her "Please Béatrice, please" and rubbing his cheek, But no, no use. She just stood there firing off a volley of exploding bullet-words, like those war novel dum-dums made to shatter in your flesh.

Did she really tell him he was going to end up drowning himself in a bottle of cat-piss wine, and that no one would even notice, because he'd become such a nothing, such a void, such a zero? That she wouldn't spend one more day with such a gutless, self-centered, ridiculous, degenerate drunk? That he was nothing but a spineless sponge, a human wreck, a dead-beat, a lush, a derelict, a wino... "Cat-piss"... Did she really use such and ugly word? "Cat-piss"...

Suddenly he hears his name. Someone calling... Like Béatrice's voice, but thundering from on high like some divine command. He's got to get up, open his eyes, fix his hair.

Footsteps, the sound of chairs pushed around, again his name called out in space, hollow, echoing like a church. He's managed to stand up, open his eyes now despite the sensation that a corkscrew is tugging his brain from his skull.

Nothing looks familiar. Nothing makes any sense in all that green.

Still, it seems to. A little... But of course it's just a dream, the last phantom of sleep. It must be. That smooth, curving wall that he's leaning against. That brownish liquid he's standing in, that he thought was a puddle but that he now sees forms a perfect ring. That convex bulge he was lying on before. Those glints of dark green, and overhead, way up, that narrow neck, that round opening, uncorked, and Béatrice's voice, outside, booming through it.

He presses his face against the glass wall, opens his eyes wide, stares out. Two feet are coming toward him, immense and bare. Deformed by the light, they look like creatures of the deep, monsters with pudgy tentacles. He seems to recall that he loved those things once, used to fondle and kiss them, found them dainty, adorable. So very English, he used to say... Beatrice's voice is thundering around him, comes surging over him in deafening waves. Then the octopus-feet scuttle off into the distance, and now, only now does he begin to yell, to scream, to pound and pound the glass wall with his fists.

She couldn't hear him. He can make out vague little rum-
blings, distant muffled echoes. She must be on the phone, complaining about him most likely.

He begins to run in ever direction, sloshes about in the dregs
of the Merlot, bumps up against the glass, tries desperately to climb
the sides, but the neck of the bottle is too far beyond his reach.

Out of breath, he falls still. He stares out at the kitchen, unrec-
ognizable, submerged in that greenish apocalyptic light, the chair legs,
the table legs, with their seaweed-like curlicues, the threatening mass of
the sideboard, seeming to move, the windowpanes, throbbing...

He would cry if he could. But no, his throat is too tight to let
even a sob escape.

Again the kitchen door opens. Béatrice comes in. She drifts
over to the gas cooker with a jellyfish gait. She makes herself a bowl
of café au lait, butters some toast. She's wearing the dress that he
bought her last year. Sounds, loud noises reach his ears, distorted,
unbearable. Béatrice has turned the radio on. For a moment he stands
looking out at her, frozen in a painful cacophony that comes pounding against the walls of glass.

She gets up, rinses out the bowl.

He hears a loud, jarring buzz. Probably someone at the door.
She turns off the radio, goes out of the room.

When she comes back in Jean-Paul is with her. They're standing almost beside him.

He begins to yell, to pound his fists, to kick... No use. Jean-
Paul has taken Béatrice in his arms. He's trying to console her.

Now she's talking about him, he can make out his name. She
casts a disheartened glance around the kitchen, shows the state that it's
in, the empty bottles lined up in the corner. Jean-Paul makes her sit

down, gives a little nod. Sadness, sympathy? Reproach? Who knows?... Now he's going to the sink, reaches underneath for a plastic garbage bag, begins stuffing it with old cigarette packs, discarded wrapping paper, the bottles...

Béatrice is sitting on her chair. She's crying.

He tells himself it's a nightmare, it must be, plunged suddenly into darkness, shaken from side to side, up and down, to the clanking of glass, bottles hitting against each other...

But down deep he knows that the dreaming was before, a sweet dream he never enjoyed to the fullest. It's the real world now he's about to pass into.

Jean-Marie Laclavetine, *Djinn*

The Authors

Alphonse Allais (1854-1905)

A charter member of the celebrated Paris cabaret Le Chat Noir, and one of the most prolific and original of the humorists of the nineties, Allais was the author of light verse, monologues, and, especially, of brief prose sketches contributed to various humor periodicals, foremost among them *Le Journal, Le Sourire*, and *Le Chat noir*. While some of his subjects appear a little dated today, his prodigious wordplay, his taste for the exaggeratedly bizarre, his off-beat, often macabre wit, and his whimsical irreverence toward the bourgeoisie in general and its technology in particular--despite his own academic training and scientific leanings--have particularly endeared him to more recent generations, and to a modern French public which, able to read his work in a number of collections, continues to consider him the undisputed master of his genre.

Guillaume Apollinaire
(pseud. Wilhelm Apollinaris de Kostrowitsky) (1880-1918)

Destined to become one of the most influential French poets of modern times, especially recognized for his influence on the Surrealists, Apollinaire was born in Rome, illegitimate son of a Vatican nobleman and a Russian mother of Polish ancestry. Educated in Monaco, he eventually found his way to Paris, where his tempestuous relationships with the prominent avant-garde writers and painters of the day--especially Picasso and Braque in their Cubist periods, and poets Max Jacob and Léon-Paul Fargue--resulted in a brief imprisonment for an alleged theft of the Mona Lisa. Enlisting in the army in 1915, he died two days before the end of World War I, leaving, in addition to several posthumous works, two important published volumes of poetry (*Alcools* and *Calligrammes*), a proto-Surrealistic verse drama (*Les Mamelles de Tirésias*), essays on art, a variety of anonymous pornography, and several collections of whimsical and picturesque prose stories.

Tristan Bernard (pseud. Paul Bernard) (1866-1947)

Born in Besançon, Bernard, a lawyer and sometime entrepreneur, spent the better and most productive part of his long life in letters. Novelist, essayist, memorialist, journalist--involved for a time in the Dreyfus debate--and comic playwright with a well-developed talent for clever plot construction and bourgeois social observation, he early honed his craft in the popular humor journal *Le Rire*, eventually becoming one of the best known and most admired humorists of the Belle Epoque and beyond. Though not without a distinctly lugubrious side, he is best remembered for his prolific output of comedies, for his famous crossword puzzle collection, and, especially, for his frequent *bons mots* and adages, tinged with an often melancholy and sardonic wit

Alexandre Breffort (1901-1971)

Jack of at least a dozen trades, Breffort had already practiced a number of them--street vendor, carnival hawker, taxi driver in the Paris of the early decades of the century--when, in 1933, he became a full-time comic author. Invited to join the staff of the then fledgeling, now venerable satirical newspaper *Le Canard enchaîné*, he was to spend the next quarter-century indulging his love of outrageous puns, celebrated among his contemporaries, in over a thousand weekly stories, as well as in poems and assorted miscellany, earning him the Prix Alphonse Allais and the Prix Scarron. One of those stories, full of the ribald flavor of the Parisian underbelly of his early days, became, first, a cabaret sketch entitled "Les Harengs terribles," and, eventually, the musical comedy and film *Irma la Douce*, translated into ten languages and known throughout the world. His resulting sudden wealth permitted him to retire and live in Switzerland, whose political climate especially agreed with his own intransigeant pacifism.

Leonora Carrington (born 1917)

A native of Lancashire, England, Carrington studied painting in London, eventually becoming involved professionally and personally with the Surrealist artist Max Ernst, with whom she moved to Paris in

1937. When Ernst was interned as an enemy alien at the beginning of World War II, she fled to Spain, where, emotionally spent, she entered a private clinic that was to provide the setting for an autobiographical account, *En bas*, written--like most of her works--in French. In 1941 she contracted a brief marriage of convenience with the Mexican poet Renato Leduc, and, after a stay in New York, settled in Mexico, where she married Hungarian photographer Imre Weisz in 1946, and where she currently makes her home. Continuing to paint throughout, Carringon early developed a style of personal, fantastic Surrealism, dominated by the representation of bizarre animals and a grotesque mythological vision. The same qualities dominate her writing, especially the brief first-person narratives of *La Dame ovale*, published in 1936 with illustrations by Ernst.

Eugène Chavette (pseud. Eugène Vachette) (1827-1902)

A tireless writer very much *à la mode* during the Second Empire, social gadabout and son of a prominent Parisian restaurateur, Chavette was author of many popular novels and light comic playlets, not all of which were of exemplary artistic quality. Potboilers aside, he found a more worthy niche in the field of journalistic humor, especially of the darkish variety, appearing in such periodicals as *Le Journal illustré*. Much admired by his contemporaries though virtually unknown today, his considerable comic talent and wit, as well as his whimsical personality, earned for him, according to one modern humor historian at least, the reputation as "one of the important ancestors of modern humor" (Carrière, p. 58).

Georges Feydeau (1863-1921)

Universally recognized as the most important and remarkable practitioner of French farce since Molière, Feydeau early exploited his comic theatrical gifts, developing his technique through a determined study of the best of his predecessors. Himself a talented actor and amateur director, from his beginnings as a youthful writer of salon monologues and one-act trifles, toast of the Paris where he was to spend his life, he blossomed into one of the most widely performed comic playwrights of his own and succeeding generations, enlivening his intricately crafted situational comedy, in some three dozen works, with not a little observation of societal and individual foibles, linguistic drollery, and a delightful lunacy that offers a generous foretaste of the latterday absurd, as well, perhaps, as of his own eventual mental breakdown. Today his name has become synonymous the world over with "French bedroom farce," though his work offers far more than that cliché implies.

Jean-Marie Laclavetine (born 1954)

A native of Bordeaux and holder of a master's degree in literature, Laclavetine has been publishing fiction--novels and short story collections--since the early 1980s, with ten important volumes to his credit. His work has been honored with no less than six literary prizes, among them the Prix Fénéon, the Prix Valéry-Larbaud, and, for *Le Rouge et le blanc*, the collection from which the present selection is taken, the prestigious Grand Prix de la Nouvelle de l'Académie Française. He is also an active translator, especially from the Italian of Giuseppe Borgese, Vittorio Brancati, Leonardo Sciascia, and others, and is currently a member of the reading committee of the Parisian publisher Gallimard.

Gabriel de Lautrec (1867-1938)

A habitué of the Quartier Latin in his youth, Lautrec, a transplant to Paris from the Midi, was already a well-known frequenter of Le Chat Noir and other humor venues of the capital before becoming a secondary-school teacher, counting among his many *fin-de-siècle* (and later) friends and acquaintances such literary luminaries as Paul Verlaine, Oscar Wilde, and Colette. His contributions to a variety of humor periodicals —*Le Rire, La Petite Semaine*, and others—as well as his translations and a study of Mark Twain, whose influence shows through in many of his stories, earned him, in the 1920s, the half-facetious, half-serious title of "Le Prince des Humoristes." He was a founding member of the equally whimsical "Académie de l'Humour Français," which included, among then prominent but lesser known honorees, Léon Xanrof and the young Jean Giraudoux.

Maurice Mac-Nab (1856-1889?)

Although admired by his contemporaries primarily as one of the more innovative of cabaret *chansonniers,* Mac-Nab, who claimed debatable descent from Scottish nobility, became best known as a leading monologuist in prose and verse. A postal official by day—as the first of his monologues in this collection attests—he was, by night, a charter member of the first Parisian "artistic" cabaret, the celebrated Club des Hydropathes, founded in 1878, and of the allied group known as Les Hirsutes. As such he rubbed shoulders with many of the literary and theatrical celebrities of the Quartier Latin: the likes of Jean Richepin, François Coppée, and the master monologuist Ernest Coquelin, known as Coquelin Cadet. When, in 1881, the Hydropathes moved to Montmartre to become the famous *café-concert* Le Chat Noir, Mac-Nab spent the last years of his life, cut short by tuberculosis, as one of its most appreciated *chansonniers,* creating—perhaps thanks to an inveterate stammer—the deadpan style that was to become that club's hallmark.

Edouard Osmont (pseud. Blaise Peti[t]v[e]au) (? - ?)

Presumed author of a notorious cabaret ditty, "Son Nombril," celebrating the particularities of a certain feminine navel, and of other Folies-Bergère numbers interpreted by Yvette Guilbert—the gangling *chanteuse* immortalized by Toulouse-Lautrec—Osmont (or Peti[t]v[e]au, since it is unclear, in fact, which was his legal name and which a pseudonym, shared, apparently, by several other humorists of the time) was one of the regular contributors to the humor magazine *Le Rire.* As such he undoubtedly had many appreciative audiences and many tens of thousands of readers in his day, since *Le Rire,* at the height of its popularity, had a circulation of some 150,000. Today, on the contrary, he is one of the forgotten; so much so that even the most rudimentary of biographical details—his dates and even his name—remain obscure. What is clear, however, is that his comic inspiration, unabashedly outrageous, as in the present monologue, opening chapter of a first-person novel, provides a prototype of turn-of-the-century *humour noir* pushed to its most extreme excesses, ridiculing as it does the perpetrator of the grotesque adventure far more than its innocent victim.

Francis [Martínez de] Picabia (1879-1953)

An avant-garde artist born in Paris of a French mother and a wealthy Cuban father attached to the Spanish government, Picabia began an eclectic painting career as an Impressionist, greatly admired by elegant Parisian society as much for his colorful personality as for his hundreds of canvases. Though no friend of Picasso's, he was nevertheless influenced by his work, passing through a Cubist period and, eventually, espousing all the various early 20th-century "isms." In trips to New York in 1913 and 1915 he was primarily responsible for introducing Dadaism into the United States. A colleague of Tristan Tzara, Picabia, between 1915 and 1920, composed several volumes of prose and poetry, in which he prefigured, to a large extent, the "automatic writing" of the Surrealists. His linguistic nihilism gave rise to a host of aphorisms for which he was famous among his contemporaries, and is well represented in *Jésus-Christ rastaquouère*, in which the present "entr'acte" appears, with little evident relation to the rest of the work.

Fernand Raynaud (1926-1973)

Like a number of celebrated post-World War II Parisian entertainers— Georges Brassens, Jacques Brel, Juliette Greco, and others—Raynaud began his all-too-brief career at the cabaret Les Trois Baudets in the shadow of Place Pigalle. Destined to become one of the most popular of his generation, he spread his witty verbal talents over a number of media, starring in Jean Nohain's long-running radio show "Trente-Six Chandelles," playing the gamut of Parisian "music-hall" theatres—the Alhambra, the Gymnase, the Variétés, et al.—and acting in a number of comic films. Author of scores of monologues and skits, a small number of which were published posthumously, he lived to see himself adulated by his public, not only in metropolitan France, but also in the French territory of New Caledonia, where he spent many of his latter years. It is ironic that a tragic automobile accident was to end the life of this light-hearted comic.

Jacques Sternberg

Born in Antwerp, Belgium, with over a score of trades and crafts to his credit, and publishing since the 1950s, Sternberg is little known in the United States despite a substantial output of novels, short stories, a play at the Comédie-Française, a film with Alain Resnais, studies on humor, science fiction, and erotica, some forty titles in all. Much of his work is in the form of brief pieces, for which he has an obvious and admitted predilection, and which, claiming inspiration from Poe, Gogol, Kafka, and Maupassant, for all their whimsy and black humor, reflect an abiding obsession with human frailty, fate, and inescapable mortality. An inveterate sailor with over 20,000 miles to his credit, he frequently injects his love of the sea into his writing, along with its potential for disaster.

Jean-Marie-Mathias-Philippe-Auguste de Villiers de l'Isle Adam (1838-1899)

With a lineage as long and impressive as his name, the Count de Villiers de l'Isle-Adam, an impoverished aristocrat who was to die a pauper's death, lived life as an anachronism. A latterday Romantic of sorts, friend of Baudelaire and admirer of Wagner for both his personal and musical extravagances, he championed the cause of idealism in all its anti-materialistic, anti-bourgeois forms, literary and artistic as well as social and political. Villiers, a sworn enemy of the egalitarian, money-based society of his day, was equally antagonistic toward the adulation of science and technology, which he saw as an evidence of soul-numbing materialistic positivism, venting his spleen in poetic and prose works of fantasy, the supernatural, biting satire, and—toward the end of his life—even science fiction. A leading practitioner of the fantastic, much influenced by Poe, his incursions into the occult were to play a considerable role in the Symbolist aesthetic.

Léon Xanrof (pseud. Léon Fourneau) (1867-1953)

When Fourneau, young lawyer and civil servant, began frequenting the cabarets of the Quartier Latin and Montmartre, his success as a composer of witty songs was such as to scandalize his properly bourgeois family, and in deference he adopted a pseudonym. Reversing the letters of the Latin *fornax* ('furnace'), a translation of *fourneau*, he thus became Xanrof, the name under which he was to be a leading incarnation of the Belle Epoque spirit throughout his long life. Eventually abandoning his position with the Ministry of Agriculture and the Court of Appeals, he devoted himself to his cabaret muse, first writing a number of short comedies and songs, and later publishing a number of collections of short stories and sketches of Parisian life and loves, all of which confirmed his popularity. Remembered today as the composer of songs made famous by Yvette Guilbert--expecially "Le Fiacre" ("Un fiacre allait trottinant, / Cahin, caha, hue-dia, hop-la!"), he also produced, in 1910, his adaptation of Oscar Strauss's operetta *Walzertraum,* under the title *Rêve de valse* ("Waltz Dream").

Bibliography

&

sources

Breton, André, *Anthologie de l'humour noir* (Paris: Editions du Sagittaire, 1950; Pauvert, 1966)

Carrière, Jean-Claude, *Anthologie de l'humour 1900* (Paris: Les Editions 1900, 1988)

Lacroix, Jean-Paul and Michel Chrestien, *Le Livre blanc de l'humour noir* (Paris: Pensée Moderne, 1966)

Poirier, René, *Cent et un contes et récits* (Paris: Librairie Gründ, 1961)

Allais, Alphonse, *Œuvres complètes*, 11 vols., ed. François Caradec (Paris: La Table Ronde, 1964-1967); includes *Œuvres anthumes* (vols. 1-3) and *Œuvres posthumes* (vols. 4-11)

Apollinaire, Guillaume, *Œuvres en prose*, 3 vols., ed. Michel Décaudin ("Bibliothèque de la Pléiade") (Paris: Gallimard, 1977)

Bernard, Tristan, *Amants et voleurs* (Paris: Flammarion, n.d.; Les Editions de France, 1932; and other publications)

——————, *Les Médecins spécialistes* (Paris: Librairie Théâtrale, 1923)

——————, *Sous toutes réserves* (Paris: Ollendorff, 1898)

Breffort, Alexandre, *Les Contes du grand-père Zig* (Paris: Editions Ergé, 1946; Editions Bellenand, 1968)

Carrington, Leonora, *La Dame ovale* (Paris: Editions GLM, 1939);

La Débutante (Paris: Flammarion, 1978)

Chavette, Eugène, *Les Petites comédies du vice* (Paris: Marpon et Flammarion, 1882)

Feydeau, Georges, *Théâtre complet*, 4 vols., ed. Henry Gidel (Paris: Garnier, 1988-1989)

Laclavetine, Jean-Marie, *Le Rouge et le blanc* (Paris: Gallimard, 1994)

Lautrec, Gabriel de, *Poèmes en prose* (Paris: Léon Vanier, 1898)

Mac-Nab, Maurice, *Poèmes mobiles et monologues* (Paris: Léon Vanier, 1886)

Osmont, Edouard (pseud. Blaise Peti[t]v[e]au), *Le Cœur sur la main et l'estomac dans les talons* (Paris, F. Juven, 1901)

Picabia, Francis, *Jésus-Christ rastaquouère* (Paris: Au Sans Pareil, 1920; reprinted in *Ecrits*, 2 vols., ed. Olivier Revault d'Allones (Paris: Belfond, 1975-1978)

Raynaud, Fernand, *Heureux!* (Paris: Editions de Provence [La Table Ronde], 1975)

Sternberg, Jacques, *Contes griffus* (Paris: Denoël, 1993)

_____, *Histoires à dormir sans vous* (Paris: Denoël, 1990)

_____, *Histoires à mourir de vous* (Paris: Denoël, 1991)

Villiers de l'Isle-Adam, Auguste de, *Contes cruels* (Paris: Calmann-Lévy, 1883; Librairie J. Corti, 1952; and other publications)

_____, *Histoires insolites* (Paris: Librairie Moderne, 1888)

Xanrof, Léon, *Pochards et pochades: histoires du Quartier Latin* (Paris: Marpon et Flammarion, 1891)

TOUR DE FARCE

A New Series of Farce Through the Ages

Translated by Norman R. Shapiro

THE PREGNANT PAUSE
or LOVE'S LABOR LOST
by Georges Feydeau

paper • ISBN: 0-936839-58-9

※

A SLAP IN THE FARCE and
A MATTER OF WIFE AND DEATH
by Eugene Labiche

paper • ISBN: 0-936839-82-1

※

THE BRAZILIAN
by Henri Meilhac
and Ludovic Halèvy

paper • ISBN: 0-936839-59-7

TOUR DE FARCE
A New Series of Farce Through the Ages

FOUR FARCES
by Georges Feydeau

TRANSLATED WITH AN INTRODUCTION
BY NORMAN R. SHAPIRO

- The plays in this volume represent the major
stages of Feydeau's career. Includes:
Wooed and Viewed
On the Marry–Go–Wrong
Not by Bed Alone
Going to Pot
*"Shapiro writes well about the edge of madness
that Feydeau's characters are always so perilous-
ly skirting ... His versions read easily. It is a
greater achievement that they seem actable."*
—TIMES LITERARY SUPPLEMENT

paper • ISBN 1-55783-305-2

TOUR DE FARCE
A New Series of Farce Through the Ages

A FLEA IN HER REAR
(or Ants in Her Pants)
and Nine Other French Farces
ENGLISH VERSIONS BY
NORMAN R. SHAPIRO

• Includes: **Allais:** The Poor Beggar and the Fairy Godmother • **Courteline:** Boubouroche, or She Dupes to Conquer • **Feydeau:** A Fitting Confusion; A Flea in Her Rear, or Ants in Her Pants; Going to Pot • **Labiche:** It's All Relative • **Meilhac and Halèvy:** Mardi Gras; Signor Nicodemo • **Sardou:** For Love or Money • **Scribe:** The Castrata

*"**THIS WONDERFUL NEW ANTHOLOGY** of plays is a rich gift to the American theatre. This volume is **A DELIGHTFUL SERVING OF DRAMATIC SEX AND CHAMPAGNE,** one which retains in English the spirit of Gay Paris in an era when an evening carriage ride to the theatre was a prelude to adventures in salacious erotica and satirical fun."*
— ROBERT SCANLAN, *BOSTON BOOK REVIEW*

paper • ISBN 1–55783–165–3